BONNIE
AND CLYDE

·····•◆•·····

The Making of a Legend

BY

KAREN BLUMENTHAL

VIKING

VIKING

An imprint of Penguin Random House LLC

375 Hudson Street

New York, New York 10014

First published in the United States of America by Viking,
an imprint of Penguin Random House LLC, 2018

LIBRARY OF CONGRESS CATALOGING-IN -PUBLICATION DATA IS AVAILABLE
ISBN 9780451471222

Printed in U.S.A.
Book design by Nancy Brennan
Set in Harriet Text

6th Printing

*Title page: Clyde and Bonnie in a photo said to be Bonnie's
favorite of her and Clyde, early 1933.*

TO MY "GANG" DURING THIS PROJECT:

Kate Park, Jo Giudice, and the amazing

and committed employees of the

Dallas Public Library

CONTENTS

———◆———

PROLOGUE

----------◆----------

BONNIE AND Clyde. For decades, they've been as famous as any pair of outlaws could be. They're the ones who adored fast cars and faster living. The dangerous young couple with undying love for each other.

JAY-Z and Beyoncé and Tupac rapped about them. Country singers from Merle Haggard to Kellie Pickler sang about them.

There have been books, a musical, and movies, especially the 1967 blockbuster *Bonnie and Clyde*. In that one, a stunning Faye Dunaway and a dimpled Warren Beatty starred as alienated outsiders trying to survive and stay together during the most difficult of times. While some reviewers hated the jolting violence, the movie was nominated for ten Academy Awards, won two Oscars, and was hailed as a breakthrough in filmmaking.

Yet, in their prime, during some of the darkest days of the Great Depression, just the mention of Clyde—and sometimes, his girlfriend, Bonnie—terrified communities and captured headlines. Their two-year crime spree spanned numerous states and included the murder of several law enforcement officers.

They are romanticized, celebrated, and remembered as the stuff of legend.

But why?

Opposite: Playing around for the camera, Bonnie pretends to lift a gun from Clyde's waistband, March 1933.

1

JOPLIN, MO., APRIL 1933.—

You've read the story of Jesse James—
Of how he lived and died;
  If you're still in need
  Of something to read
Here's the story of Bonnie and Clyde.

—Bonnie Parker, "The Story of Bonnie and Clyde"

IN TRUTH, Bonnie Parker was just messing around the day her most famous photo was taken.

But once a picture runs over and over again in newspapers all across the country, people draw their own conclusions.

By 1930s standards, this shot was a doozy. Bonnie, twenty-two years old and

Bonnie poses with a gun and a cigar, March 1933. This is the photograph that made her famous.

maybe a nick under five feet tall, propped her heel on the bumper of a car in a most unladylike position. She held a revolver stolen from a police officer on her hip. Most outrageous, she clenched a cigar between her teeth, something a decent woman would *never* do. Her expression was defiant.

In reality, she had borrowed the cigar from her friend W. D. Jones and was playing around for the camera. She knew how to shoot, sure, but she rarely fired a gun in public. She would never actually smoke a cigar; she wasn't *that* type of woman. She did smoke cigarettes, though—lots of people did in those dreary days of the Great Depression.

When the photo was snapped, Bonnie and her boyfriend, Clyde Barrow, had been running from police for about a year. Clyde was already wanted for robbery and at least four murders in Texas and Oklahoma, where he was considered an elusive and extremely dangerous criminal with a quick trigger finger. But beyond the region, he wasn't well known. To law enforcement and reporters, Bonnie was only a female companion along for the ride as they raced through New Mexico, Texas, Oklahoma, Missouri, and Arkansas.

Then they decided to take a break in Joplin, Missouri.

On April 1, 1933, Bonnie, Clyde, and W. D., a teenager who had been a family friend of the Barrows, moved to a two-bedroom garage apartment. They were looking forward to a reunion with Clyde's older brother Buck, who had just gotten out of a Texas prison, and Buck's wife, Blanche.

A neighbor, noticing that the curtains were always drawn, grew suspicious. Thinking they were thieves or bootleggers, he contacted the police, who began to watch the apartment.

In the late afternoon of April 13—the day before the group planned to leave—Clyde and W. D. were in the garage when five officers pulled up in two cars. When the county constable emerged with a gun, the two outlaws quickly responded with a hail of bullets. The constable was hit in the neck and shoulder. Another barrage of buckshot hit a Joplin detective.

In the intense gunfight, W. D. took a bullet in his side and Clyde was struck in the chest, which left him bleeding but not badly injured. Somehow, the gang managed to pile into a stolen car and escape the bloody scene.

The county constable was dead. The other lawman was dying.

Inside the apartment, amid partially packed clothes and dishes dirty from lunch, police found Buck and Blanche's marriage license, Clyde's guitar, and a poem that Bonnie was refining and recopying, the ink still wet. In Blanche's bag, there was something else: a camera and undeveloped film.

Soon after, Bonnie Parker's photos appeared for the first time in the newspapers. There was the outrageous one with the cigar, and another one, where she teasingly poked a rifle into Clyde's midsection, pretending to lift his gun. There were plenty of pictures of Clyde and W. D., too. But Bonnie's photos were the attention grabbers.

Once the photographs were public, Bonnie was no longer merely a criminal's girlfriend—or, to use the derogatory term, *moll*—along for the ride. She was a partner, a gang member, a rare female fugitive with a known name and a *really* bad reputation. It was almost too scandalous to believe.

LEGEND HAS IT: OUTLAW FASHION

While their crimes put Clyde and Bonnie in the headlines, their fashion choices set them apart from other lawbreakers in the news. In photos, Clyde often had on a suit and a fashionable fedora, and Bonnie often wore dresses and popular berets or cloche hats, which fit snug to the head.

Clyde didn't always wear a tie and Bonnie didn't always have on a short bolero jacket and long skirt. But when a camera was out or they wanted to impress the public, they found a way to sport current styles. By the 1930s, straight flapper silhouettes had given way to slim dresses with broad shoulders and small waists, and more and more people were buying outfits "ready to wear" from a store, rather than sewing them at home. Both men and women wore hats.

Underneath her hats, Bonnie had a modern short hairstyle with finger curls, waves created by crimping wet hair. She frequently wore makeup, which was just beginning to be popular, especially with young women.

As detectives began to follow their trail, they found plain calico housedresses and men's shorts left behind in abandoned cars and hideouts. But officers also found receipts for purchases made by Barrow family members. One, from Lord's dress shop in Dallas, was for a green angora wool dress with a small scarf and matching green belt. It cost $6.95, or about $130 in today's dollars.

At a time when many Americans could barely afford food and shelter, the couple's clothes left the impression that crime paid very well.

Among the other Depression-era bandits who captured the public's attention during those dark years, John Dillinger was smoother and more famous. Baby Face Nelson was meaner. Pretty Boy Floyd was more Robin Hood–like, sharing his ill-gotten wealth with others in need. But Clyde Barrow and Bonnie Parker were something else altogether: outlaws in love.

To young people in the region trying to get by during the toughest of times, Clyde and Bonnie seemed to be living the life—at least based on those photos left behind in Joplin. Though a slight man, roughly five feet six inches tall, and a slender one hundred thirty-five pounds, Clyde was dapper in a suit and fedora. Petite Bonnie, weighing less than one hundred pounds soaking wet, was fashionably dressed, her hair carefully tucked in a beret-like hat.

"Their whole image was one of glamour," recalled Jim Wright, a longtime Texas congressman who was a kid living in the region at the time. "You rather imagined them holed up in some upscale hotel," he said. "It was a very romantic existence we felt they must enjoy. And even if you did not approve of them, you would still have to envy them a little, to be so good-looking and rich and happy."

In truth, their families said, there was little joy for them. Their world had become a "living hell."

2

TELICO, TEX., MARCH 24, 1909.—

They call them cold-blooded killers;
They say they are heartless and mean;
But I say this with pride,
That I once knew Clyde
When he was honest and upright and clean.

—Bonnie Parker, "The Story of Bonnie and Clyde"

IF HE had been born in a different time or place, Clyde Barrow might have been a musician, a car mechanic, or a race car driver. Bonnie Parker might have starred on the stage. But a whole mess of rough circumstances and terrible choices took them in another direction, beginning in their earliest years.

Clyde's parents, Henry Barrow and Cumie Walker, came from modest circumstances, but they had big plans when they married on December 5, 1891, near Swift, a small farming community in East Texas. Cumie had just turned seventeen and Henry was eighteen. "Everything looked bright and rosey then," Cumie wrote later. "We had dreams of some day owning a farm of our own."

They rented a farm nearby. Elvin, who was called Jack, was born in 1894, followed by a daughter, Artie, in 1899. "We soon awoke to a realization that life was indeed earnest. As our family grew this became more and more apparent, and we had no time then for day dreaming," Cumie wrote. "We found that life was very much of a struggle most of the time, although sometimes we got along fairly well."

Hoping for better land, the growing family moved to another farm in East Texas. There, Marvin Ivan, nicknamed Buck, was born in 1903, and Nell was born in 1905.

The Barrow family (in Texas, their name was typically pronounced *BEAR-a* rather than *BEAR-o)* still struggled to grow cotton and other crops and to make ends meet. They moved again, this time to another rural area called Telico. The population was tiny, likely less than fifty people, but it was near the larger town of Ennis and about forty miles southeast of Dallas, a young city sitting on several rail lines.

Clyde Chestnut Barrow was the fifth child. His birthday was March 24, but the actual year is unclear. It is officially recorded as 1909—but his mother wrote 1910 in the family Bible, which some family members considered the true date. L. C. came along in 1913 and Marie, the seventh and last child, was born in 1918, when Jack and Artie were already grown.

As a child, Clyde was "a good boy, playful and full of life," his mother recalled. Like all kids, he got into trouble occasionally. A local storekeeper caught him dipping into a candy jar. Rather than punish the boy, he required Clyde to whistle when he was in the store, to be sure he wasn't enjoying more treats.

Clyde was so close to L. C. and Nell that the family nicknamed him Bud, a shortened version of buddy. When he wasn't picking cotton or doing other work on the farm, he loved to play. He and

L. C. shot marbles, or Clyde pretended to be Jesse James or one of his gang members, famous outlaws who robbed banks and trains in the 1870s, and who were often portrayed in the movies and in cheap novels as folk heroes. When his big sister Nell wanted to take the lead role, young Clyde balked and refused to play. Westerns were also a big hit at the Telico movie house, and the Barrow children were happy to walk the three miles there to escape in a Saturday matinee if they could scrounge up the few pennies to get in.

Clyde loved to dance and sing, and, his mother recalled, "He liked music better than anything." He taught himself to play guitar and later danced a sharp Charleston. "His first ambition," his mother said, "was to be in some kind of a band with other boys."

All of the kids learned to use a gun, and Cumie remembered Clyde was a good shot. But as an animal lover, he wasn't fond of hunting, preferring instead to shoot at cans and other targets.

The Barrows never were able to make a comfortable living off the land. The family lived in a three-room shack that was so small that most of the family slept on makeshift pallets on the floor. Nell recalled that they rarely had enough to eat or much in the way of clothes, even when cotton prices tripled during and just after World War I, from 1915 to 1919.

To make up for what their farm didn't produce, Henry and Cumie often worked for others, following the harvest from farm to farm as migrant workers. While they were on the road, the younger children were sent for up to three months at a time to an uncle's farm about twenty-five miles to the south. There, they worked in the fields, just like at home, but also enjoyed playing with their cousins and going fishing. At their uncle's, there was

Clyde Barrow (center) and L. C. Barrow (second from left) in an undated school photo in Telico.

adequate food on the table.

Cumie pushed her kids to go to church and sent them off to school as often as possible, although usually that was only after they'd done their work on the farm. Their father, Henry, had been sickly as a child, suffering from chills and fevers, and spent a total of one half day at school, never learning to read or write. Their mother wanted more for her own clan.

Some of the children did better than others. Clyde enjoyed the church's Sunday school and was as consistent as any of the kids about going to school. Buck, the third child, however, preferred being outdoors and made it only through third grade before he began skipping classes regularly. Like his dad, he never really learned to read or write.

The Barrows' tough times grew worse after the war. Prices for cotton and other crops plunged as Europe got back to business, making it even more difficult for the family to scrape together enough to live on.

By then, the oldest son, Jack, had married and become a car mechanic in Dallas, working out of the back of his home. Artie had become a hairdresser in the city, and Nell married and joined

LEGEND HAS IT: FAMOUS OUTLAWS

In an era before movie stars and sports icons, notorious outlaws— such as Jesse James and Billy the Kid—were thought of as heroes by many Americans. They were celebrated in inexpensive magazines and dime novels that sensationalized their exploits and portrayed them as brave and daring men who challenged authority. Pretending to be the Jesse James gang the way Clyde Barrow and his siblings did was common for kids.

Jesse James, born in 1847 in Clay County, Missouri, was known as a murderous robber of trains and banks, supposedly in revenge for mistreatment at the hands of Northerners after the Civil War. Billy the Kid, born William Henry McCarty, Jr., around 1860, had a reputation as a quick-shooting cattle rustler and thief.

Both died young and became far more famous from the retelling and remaking of their stories than from their actual crimes. Movies transformed them into rebellious, romanticized larger-than-life characters. Their stories were endlessly engrossing, combining fear, fascination, gore, and glamour in a way that riveted viewers and turned the bad guys into cultural legends.

her. Buck had grown antsy and followed his siblings.

As they reached their late forties, Henry and Cumie saw fewer possibilities for farmers. So they packed up what little they had and headed to the big city with four-year-old Marie, nine-year-old L. C., and Clyde on the edge of his teen years. The move would change their lives in ways they could never have imagined.

3

WEST OF DALLAS, TEX., 1922.—

———◦———

From Irving to West Dallas viaduct
Is known as the Great Divide,
Where the women are kin,
And the men are men,
And they won't "stool" on Bonnie and Clyde.

—Bonnie Parker, "The Story of Bonnie and Clyde"

IN 1922, when the Barrows arrived with their horse and wagon, Dallas was a budding city of about 160,000 residents with one foot in the twentieth century and one firmly stuck in its Southern past.

The city and the communities around it were strictly segregated by race, with separate neighborhoods, schools, and entrances for whites and blacks. The racist Ku Klux Klan was on the rise, terrorizing African Americans and orchestrating the firings of Jews and Catholics who held prominent positions. Its members included city business leaders, government officials, and even the police chief.

At the same time, the downtown was becoming more modern every day. On Elm Street, the ornate Majestic Theatre opened in 1921 to host vaudeville shows and movies, and the elegant Magnolia Building, boasting twenty-nine stories, joined other skyscrapers the next year.

Across the United States, these years would become known as the Roaring Twenties because of the explosion in music, movies, and dance. Radio brought news and entertainment into people's homes; real estate and stock prices soared; many families bought their first car; and women, now empowered with the vote, claimed more rights. But even as many Americans grew wealthier, up to four out of every ten Americans were poor, earning barely enough for food and shelter. Current and former Southern farmers, both black and white, were among those hurting the most.

As Dallas newcomers, the Barrows initially camped with other destitute families under one of the long bridges that ran from downtown across the narrow Trinity River. The city wasn't fond of the "idle farm hands," as one Dallas newspaper called them, who had come to Dallas desperate for work. These families were often urged to relocate to West Dallas, an unincorporated area just outside the city limits near the Trinity River bottoms. There, in the shadow of the city's ornate office buildings, were the poorest of the poor, an underclass that was largely invisible to the city's other residents.

In truth, invisible and ignored was better than others had it at the time. In those same river bottoms, the Ku Klux Klan rounded up at least sixty-eight blacks, Catholics, Jews, and immigrants in the spring of 1922 and flogged them, ordering some to leave town.

From the bridge, the Barrows moved to a squatters' campground, where they lived under their wagon for a time, eventually adding tents. Some West Dallas residents found factory jobs, but Henry Barrow used the wagon and the family's horse to collect junk and scrap metal and sell it to neighborhood salvage yards. Clyde and his older brother Buck sometimes helped out by steal-

A 1920s-era Dallas scrap peddler. Henry Barrow's horse and cart probably looked similar to this one.

ing metal their father could resell. It was likely their first taste of petty crime.

The conditions were dreadful. So much raw sewage was dumped in the Trinity River that in 1925 the State Health Department said it looked like "some mythological river of death." At least a couple of waste dumps dotted the area. A nearby cement plant and other factories spewed acrid smoke into the air, while oil and chemical refineries operated open-air lagoons to contain spills. Most of the roads in Dallas were paved, but the roads in West Dallas were dirt or gravel. When it rained, they dissolved into mud. If spring rains were especially heavy, the whole area flooded and families had to escape to higher ground.

Both money and food were scarce. Many days, the family had to rely on charities that brought bologna sandwiches—dubbed "West Dallas round steak"—or sometimes just stale bread to the campground. Christmas presents were usually nothing more than fruit, nuts, and candy from the Salvation Army.

In early 1923, Flora Saylor, the social welfare superintendent for Dallas's United Charities, described the campground as a colony of at least twenty families living in "tattered wagons and improvised huts," without proper bedding or enough food. "Sanitary conditions at the camp are terrible," she said.

Diseases like typhoid fever and diphtheria were a constant concern. At one point, Clyde, Marie, and their father got so sick that they were all admitted to a local hospital.

Hattie Rankin Moore, a Dallas church volunteer who became devoted to the neighborhood, later would note that many young men from West Dallas often had few options beyond mischief. "We have no parks, no playgrounds, no handy schools, no lights, no water, no gas," she said. "The dogs in Dallas are housed better than our boys and girls." In fact, much of West Dallas wouldn't get electricity, running water, and indoor toilets until the early 1950s.

Despite the squalid conditions, people in West Dallas took care of one another. "You didn't have to lock your door because you didn't have anything to steal and nobody would take it from you anyway," said Eddie Shores, who was a few years younger than Clyde. There might not be food in your house, he added, "but if your neighbor had a pot of beans going, you knew you could get a bite to eat."

Clyde was in and out of West Dallas. In the early months after his family moved there, he lived off and on with his uncle's family and chose to be baptized at fourteen at the Eureka, Texas, Baptist church. When he was home, Cumie tried to keep him in school, but he never attended regularly after the family left the farm. There were far more young people to hang out with, cool places to go, money to make, and girls. Whatever Clyde did with his life, a sixth-grade education would have to do.

As a young man, he didn't have much trouble finding places to work in Dallas, though wages were low. Clyde started at the Brown Cracker & Candy Company for a dollar a day, moving on to the Procter & Gamble soap factory, where he earned 30 cents an hour, equal to about $4 an hour today. He jumped from job to job in search of higher pay, working briefly as an usher at the Palace Theater, at the Nu Grape Bottling Company, United Glass Company, and A&K Auto Top and Paint Shop.

During these years, Cumie and Henry Barrow scraped and saved lumber and nails to build a small shack on a plot a few blocks from the campground. When Clyde was working, he often stayed in East Dallas with his sister Nell, who had married around 1925. Her husband worked during the day, but was a bandleader at night, and he taught his musical brother-in-law to play the saxophone. Clyde's first weeks with the instrument were rough on the ears and painful for the neighbors. But he practiced for hours, and when he mastered the sax, it became his favorite instrument.

Clyde and his older brothers and sisters shared some of

A teenage Clyde with his sisters Nell (left) and Artie in the late 1920s.

their paychecks with their struggling parents. "He would sometimes give me some of the money he earned, but most of the time he would buy me something," Cumie remembered.

As Clyde moved deeper into his teen years, Cumie noticed a change in her once-playful Bud. He increasingly focused on his clothes and appearance, favoring much dressier clothes than he would have ever worn on the farm. He was rarely happy with his income, feeling like he needed to make more.

Clyde with his girlfriend Eleanor Williams, 1926.

She blamed this new frustration on "wayward women in the neighborhood." (To Cumie, that might just be a young woman who was fond of lipstick and rouge, something she strongly opposed.)

The pursuit of one of his first loves was also the first time Clyde got in serious trouble. He fell for a girl named Eleanor and liked her enough to have her initials, EBW, tattooed on his left forearm. (Later, Clyde would adopt an alias, Elvin Williams, using those initials.)

After a disagreement in late 1926, Eleanor took off to East Texas to see relatives. Clyde decided to pick her up and bring her back. He rented a car and took Eleanor's mother along. But he stayed in East Texas and kept the car longer than he was supposed to. The owner reported it stolen and when police went to fetch it, Clyde hid from them.

In a move that pretty much ended his chances of winning over Eleanor's parents, Clyde headed home, leaving both his girlfriend and her mother behind. Later, he was arrested for theft and jailed. Because the car was recovered, the charges were eventually dropped.

Soon after, Clyde and Buck were caught with a truckload of stolen turkeys. Buck took the blame and Clyde narrowly avoided another lockup.

By the late 1920s, Clyde had acquired a new set of friends and was learning new skills. Among them was stealing cars. Thanks to Henry Ford's inexpensive Model Ts and Model As and General Motors' willingness to let people pay off a new car over time, four out of five families owned a car by the end of the decade. Hundreds of thousands of miles of roads had been paved, including new cross-country highways.

But crime had also picked up. Cars gave bank robbers an easy getaway and helped bootleggers transport illegal liquor during Prohibition, a time when selling alcohol was illegal. Clyde and his friends tapped into an emerging trade in stolen cars. Many owners made theft especially easy by leaving their keys in them.

Between stealing cars, burglary, and a developing talent for cracking safes, Clyde put himself on the radar of the Dallas police department. Dallas officers weren't thrilled about traipsing into poverty-stricken West Dallas, outside the city limits, so they often went to Clyde's work to pick him up for questioning about local crimes. "Whenever a car was stolen, or a house was burglarized, the police would drag him downtown,"

Clyde's interest in cars and clothes deepened in the mid-1920s.

recalled a friend of Eleanor's. "Of course, he was never charged with anything, but they'd beat him up and try to make him confess to things he'd never done."

Hoping to turn down the heat, Clyde began to ply his criminal trades outside of Dallas. Still, the extra police attention made it hard to keep a job and made him increasingly angry and distrustful of authority. "After he was picked up so many times he just came to have a hatred for the law, and figured it didn't do much, if any, good to try to do right," his mother wrote later.

———○———

While Clyde Barrow was winning and losing girlfriends and becoming well acquainted with the police, Bonnie Parker was falling in love.

Born in Rowena, in the western part of Texas, on October 1, 1910, Bonnie was the middle child of Charles and Emma Krause Parker, between her older brother, Buster, and younger sister, Billie Jean. Her mother remembered her as "a beautiful baby, with cotton colored curls, the bluest eyes you ever saw, and an impudent little red mouth." Her father was a bricklayer and the family regularly attended the local Baptist church.

When Bonnie was four, her father died suddenly. Emma packed up the three kids and moved into her parents' small farm in West Dallas, near an area known as Cement City, a company town of a few hundred people surrounding a smoke-spewing cement plant. Emma went to work as a seamstress in a factory while her mother watched the children. On Sundays, they all walked to a Baptist church downtown.

Bonnie was a handful, eager to act up for attention. Though her grandmother sometimes spanked her with a hairbrush, she wasn't easy to keep in line. Like Clyde, she was musical. Emma gave all three children piano lessons, but let Bonnie stop when it was clear that she could play whatever she heard by ear.

At school, she was a quick learner with a flair for the dramatic. In 1922, when she was eleven, Bonnie competed in the Dallas County literary contest and won the elementary spelling competition. Her win helped her school walk away with a surprise championship against bigger, much-richer neighborhoods.

Bonnie's blonde hair and blue eyes attracted boys, who tried to woo her with gifts of candy and chewing gum. At the same time, she had a quick temper and regularly got into fights with both boys and girls. Despite the trouble she could cause, she was popular with the drama teacher, who spotted a knack for writing and making speeches and cast her in school plays and musical shows.

Bonnie enjoyed those roles more than almost anything. On Saturdays, she often went fishing with her sister, Billie, who was three years younger. Bonnie much preferred performing to catching a potential dinner. "I'd tell her 'Be quiet!' I couldn't catch any fish," Billie said later.

Bonnie waved off her complaints. "When I'm on Broadway and I have my name in lights, you'll be sorry you talked to me like that," she told her sister.

Girls from West Dallas might have big dreams, but they didn't have many options. Most of them married very young, dropped out of school, and got a job. Bonnie was no exception.

At fifteen, she fell head over heels in love with Roy Thornton, a tall, handsome classmate. She had their names tattooed inside hearts on her upper right thigh. Though her mother was reluctant, Bonnie convinced her to consent to their marriage. Bonnie and Roy were married on September 25, 1926, a week before her sixteenth birthday.

The youthful romance was rocky from the start. The newlyweds rented a place about two blocks from her family, but Bonnie pined for her mother. Every evening, she demanded that Roy take her back to her mother's home. The visits were so frequent that Emma Parker actually felt sorry for Roy, "who was having a lot of difficulty with his honeymoon."

Within weeks of their marriage, Bonnie and Roy had moved back in with Emma in a rental home in Dallas, which suited both of them, Emma said later.

After less than a year of marriage, however, Roy began disappearing for stretches at a time—ten days in August 1927, nearly three weeks in October, and then in December, for weeks on end. In a diary entry on January 1, 1928, seventeen-year-old Bonnie wrote, "I wish to tell you that I have a roaming husband with a roaming mind." Though she loved him and missed him, "I am not going to take him back," she insisted.

Over the next several days, she bided her time, going to silent movies like *A Night of Love, Afraid to Love,* and *The Primrose Path,* and going on dates with other men. But she yearned for Roy. "Sure am lonesome," she noted one day. "Sure am blue tonight," she wrote on another. Roy apparently had become a heavy drinker and turned

Bonnie with her husband, Roy Thornton, circa 1926.

to crime. He did show back up in early 1929 but—as she had promised—Bonnie sent him away for good. A few months later, he was arrested and convicted of burglary and sentenced to the state penitentiary. Bonnie never saw her husband again. But she made a deliberate decision not to seek a divorce. She told her mother that she didn't think it was fair to do that while he was in prison. She continued to wear her wedding ring.

During Roy's absence, Bonnie landed a job as a waitress at Hargrave's Café. She was energetic and charming, and her outgoing personality made her popular, which likely helped her earn a little more in tips. In 1929, Bonnie switched jobs and went to work at a café near the courthouse downtown. Lawyers and judges ate there regularly, as did downtown businessmen. Ted Hinton, who would later spend years trying to catch her as a

*A glamorous
portrait of a
teenage Bonnie,
mid-1920s.*

sheriff's deputy, recalled that she had a ready quip and an ability to casually flirt with customers. "Bonnie could turn heads," he said.

In October 1929, the stock market crashed, pushing the nation into a financial tailspin. As investors lost billions of dollars in stock investments almost overnight, businesses and governments quickly began to let employees go. The newly unemployed cut back as well, on everything from laundry to eating out. The number of Americans out of work skyrocketed. The café near the courthouse closed in November, and Bonnie joined the millions who had lost their jobs. Though she looked and looked, she couldn't find another one.

In January 1930, she was at her brother and sister-in-law's house in West Dallas when a dark-haired young man named Clyde Barrow came to visit. The two were immediately attracted to each other. Clyde saw in Bonnie Parker a tiny, lively, beautiful young woman. She saw a slight, well-dressed fellow who was good-looking and quietly confident. They quickly became a couple.

Just a few weeks later, Clyde stopped by the Parker residence to see Bonnie. Emma Parker said that she found Clyde likeable and very handsome, "with his dark wavy hair, dancing brown eyes, and a dimple that popped out now and then when he smiled." She thought he looked like a young law student or doctor. "He had what they call charm," she said. "He was good company, and full of fun, always laughing and joking. I could see why Bonnie liked him."

Clyde stayed so late that Emma invited him to spend the night and loaned him a pair of Bonnie's brother's pajamas.

Clyde Barrow was still snoozing on the couch when the police arrived the next day. They had been looking for him and guessed that he would be with his girlfriend.

They didn't count on her reaction. Bonnie hollered and wept and held on to Clyde, begging the officers leave him alone. "I thought she was going crazy," her mother remembered.

Clyde tried to reassure her, but that didn't help. Despite her best efforts, the police took Clyde to jail. It was an unusual start to a most unusual love affair.

4

WACO, TEX., MARCH 1930.—

But the laws fooled around,
Kept taking him down
And locking him up in a cell,
Till he said to me,
"I'll never be free,
So I'll meet a few of them in hell."

—Bonnie Parker, "The Story of Bonnie and Clyde"

THE DALLAS police held Clyde for a few days and then sent him to Denton, about forty miles to the northwest. Turns out Clyde had been exceptionally busy before he started romancing Bonnie: he was wanted in at least three towns for burglaries and car thefts.

In late 1929, just a couple of months before he met Bonnie, Clyde, his brother Buck, and a friend had stolen a car, burglarized a home, and lifted a safe from a Denton garage. An officer saw them and tried to stop their car. In his rush, Clyde smashed into a curb, breaking an axle. All three young men spilled out of the car and ran.

The officer fired on them and Buck was hit in both thighs,

badly injured, but not critically. The friend was caught as well. Clyde, however, managed to escape and hide overnight before making his way back to West Dallas unscathed.

Buck and the friend had already been convicted of the crime and sent to prison. Now, following his arrest at Bonnie's, Clyde was facing time, too.

While Clyde was in the Dallas and Denton jails, Bonnie composed long, dramatic letters to him that swung between declaring her love and worrying about how much time he would serve. "I have had the blues so bad all day that I could lie right down and die," she wrote. "Sugar, when you do get out, I want you to go to work, and for God's sake, don't get into any more trouble."

In another letter, she wrote about going downtown and learning Clyde had been transferred to Denton. "I was so blue and mad and discouraged, I just had to cry. I had maybelline on my eyes and it began to stream down my face," she wrote. She stopped the car and put her "head down on the steering wheel and sure did boohoo."

Later in the letter, she added a little drama to her despair, worrying that Clyde might get twenty-five years of punishment and solitary confinement.

"Wouldn't that be terrible?" she wrote.

Denton officials decided they didn't have enough evidence to charge him. But Waco, about one hundred miles south of Dallas, was waiting for him. In March, Clyde was transferred to the county jail there to be tried for stealing cars and burglarizing a business.

Bonnie was determined to follow him, arguing with her mother until she got permission to go. She and Clyde's mother,

Cumie, traveled together to Waco, staying with Bonnie's cousin Mary. Bonnie was thrilled to see Clyde for the first time in two weeks and visited him at least once a day at the jail, even after his mother returned to Dallas.

In Waco, the wheels of justice spun quickly. On March 3, the young man the newspapers nicknamed "Schoolboy" for his youthful appearance, was charged with seven crimes.

Two days later, without a lawyer present, Clyde pleaded guilty and was sentenced to two years for each charge; the judge agreed to let him serve them all at the same time, rather than a total of fourteen years. Like others convicted of serious crimes, he was supposed to be sent from the county jail to a state-run prison to serve his time.

But at the same time Clyde arrived in Waco, state prison officials closed their doors to newly convicted inmates. The Texas prisons were overflowing and men were sleeping on the floor between beds. The main state prison at Huntsville had been built for 650, but now housed 950 men.

Just weeks before, Texas governor Dan Moody had declared that the prison was "not a fit place for human habitation."

"I have a dog, and I think a lot of that dog," he told the state legislature, "but I'd kill him before I'd put him down there to stay."

For the time being, convicted criminals would remain in city and county jails.

The reprieve gave Clyde and two cellmates, William Turner and Emery Abernathy, some time to think about their predicament and devise a plan.

On the evening of March 11, less than a week after they had

An early Dallas Police Department mug shot of Clyde, possibly from 1926.

all been sentenced, Turner asked a jailer for a bottle of milk. When the jailer opened the door and stepped in, Turner blocked the doorway and Abernathy rushed toward the jailer with a gun he had mysteriously acquired. They grabbed the jailer's keys and Clyde, Turner, and Abernathy pushed their way out of the cell, locking the jailer inside.

They ran down the stairs and overpowered a jailer stationed at the bottom, stealing his keys as well. Then they let themselves out of the jail, disappearing into the night. Within minutes, they had stolen a car and headed west. By daybreak, they had stolen and abandoned at least four cars.

Police called every big city in Texas looking for them, without success. Then, after a week on the loose, the young men made an embarrassing mistake a thousand miles away in Middletown, Ohio, a community about halfway between Cincinnati and Dayton. They had "worked the town all night long, until nearly 4 o'clock in the morning," Abernathy said. By "work," he meant looting and pillaging: they had robbed three filling stations, cleaned out a women's clothing store of silk apparel, and hit a railroad ticket office, walking away with $57.50, the equivalent of about $830 today.

With Clyde at the wheel, they tried to head out of town. But the winding roads and dark night confused him. Four hours later, they drove past the railroad station again. Police were still there investigating, and they recognized the car's license plate number, which a witness had provided earlier.

Officers quickly pursued them, firing into the air. Turner and Abernathy jumped out of the car and gave themselves up. Clyde, however, took off. He managed to elude the police for more than an hour before he was cornered near a riverbank. After exchanging a few shots with the police, Clyde tossed the gun from the jailbreak into the water and surrendered.

Inside the car, police found the trappings of seasoned criminals. In addition to cans of beans, there were burglary tools and license plates from several states. The young men simply hadn't gotten around to changing their license plate after such a busy night.

The newspapers ridiculed their clumsiness. "Baby Thugs Captured," crowed the big headline in the *Waco News-Tribune*, saying that Clyde was only seventeen. "Waco's Dumbell Bandits, Captured in Ohio, Back in M'Lennan County Jail," mocked the *Waco Sunday Tribune,* which went on to call them the "baby dumbells." That paper said baby-faced Clyde was eighteen years old, though he was actually almost twenty or twenty-one—depending on which birth year you believe.

The jailers were not amused at all. The three escapees were placed alone in a more secure area on the third floor of the jail and no visitors were allowed.

Judge Richard J. Munroe, who had given Clyde a fairly lenient term, was downright angry. On Clyde's birthday, March 24, he lambasted the young man and his partners.

"I have lost my patience trying to help these men who keep getting into trouble. They get on the sympathy of the juries, a suspended sentence or a long sentence to be run concurrently is recommended, then they break jail," the judge said.

If they continued with their criminal careers, he warned, they would end up facing the ultimate penalty: execution in Texas's electric chair.

"I think it would be a good thing to save you boys from the chair, eventually, to send you up for long terms," he told them. "You are liable to go round here shooting a peace officer, if you can shoot straight. You keep breaking into houses, and some of these days, you're going to either get shot or shoot somebody else. With the records you've got, you'd probably get the chair when you were tried."

With that, he sentenced them all to longer prison terms—fourteen years in Clyde's case, or two years for each of his seven crimes.

Officials in Waco were eager to get the criminals out of their jails, especially after they learned that the locks on the inner cell doors holding Clyde and his friends had been jimmied so they wouldn't work. But the state prison's NO OCCUPANCY sign was still up.

McLennan County sheriff Leslie Stegall called the head of the state penitentiary commission to plead his case. "Listen," he said, "I've got a bunch of bad hombres up here, lifers and things like that. They've already broken out once." And, he added, his head jailer had taken a three months' leave of absence because his blood pressure had soared after the jailbreak.

"Can't you take a few of them off my hands?" he begged.

"Sorry" came the reply. "You'll have to worry along as best you can till we get rid of a few boarders."

Clyde's case was complicated by a new development: officials in Houston decided he might be responsible for a murder back in July 1929, and charged him with the crime.

"Horse feathers," Clyde responded when told. He insisted he was in Dallas at the time and knew nothing about the murder.

Still, he was to be transferred soon to Houston to stand trial. His mother asked to see him again before he was moved farther away. While there, she gave an interview to the *Waco News-Tribune*. Cumie Barrow may have been poor and poorly educated, but she was a loving and intensely protective mother—and an impressively savvy advocate for her son.

"Clyde was just eighteen last Monday," she told the reporter, dropping at least two years from his true age.

"He never has been in any serious trouble before. He was arrested once in Dallas and once in Fort Worth on suspicion, but they let him go," she said, leaving out the family's knowledge that he had clearly been up to no good for some time. "He was working hard, paying for an automobile, when he got into these scrapes with the Waco boys."

She said she didn't know her son had a gun when he was

caught in Ohio. This seemingly surprised her, even though he grew up on farms where guns were common. "He never had much to do with guns, and I'm sure he isn't a good shot," his mother said. "I'm glad he isn't."

She was also certain that he wasn't in Houston at the time of the murder. "I have receipts showing regular payments he was making on an automobile at the time he is said to have been in Houston," she added.

The paper reported that Cumie brought along a young woman who said she was a friend of Clyde's—presumably Bonnie Parker. The friend "appeared amused," the paper said, at the story of the cell door locks being broken.

Ultimately, Clyde didn't have to go to Houston. In late March, police found a more likely suspect and the murder charges against Clyde were dropped. But it wasn't until April 21 that the "one-way wagon" showed up at the county jail. Clyde was handcuffed and chained to his fellow prisoners by the neck for the trip southeast to a new life in the Texas prison system.

———————————

At the time Clyde left the Waco jail, officials didn't know where the gun used in the jailbreak had come from. Initially they guessed it had been smuggled in with some food. When the three young offenders returned from Ohio, they claimed they had gotten it from black prisoners confined in the segregated side of the jail. The truth was something else altogether.

Security at the jail was fairly lax, and on one of Bonnie's visits, Clyde passed along a request from William Turner. Turner lived in East Waco with his mother and sister. There was a gun

Bonnie working as a waitress, circa 1929.

in the house, but Turner didn't want to get his mom or sister in trouble by asking them to bring it to him. He and Clyde wanted Bonnie to get it and bring it to them.

Turner scribbled a map on a rough piece of tablet paper, showing where to find the house key and where the gun and ammunition were hidden. Under the drawing, Clyde had written, "You are the sweetiest baby in the world to me. I love you."

Bonnie agreed to help, and took her cousin Mary along. They found the key easily, but the gun wasn't where it was supposed to be. They turned the house upside down looking for it, tossing items from drawers and dressers until they finally found it hidden in a window seat. Leaving the house looking like a tornado had just touched down, they returned to Mary's.

Mary was terrified about what they had done and what Bonnie was about to do—but she recalled that Bonnie wasn't rattled at all. Using a hidden belt, Bonnie slipped the gun into a makeshift pocket between her breasts. She figured the jailers wouldn't try to pat down a young woman there.

They returned to the jail, and Bonnie asked to see Clyde, promising to be quick.

While Mary sat sweating with fear in a waiting area, Bonnie greeted Clyde, passing the gun to him. They chatted for a few minutes and then she left.

She and Mary returned to Mary's home, locking the doors and shutting the shades. Mary worried about what they had done, and they both fretted about Clyde. The next morning, after Bonnie read in the newspapers that Clyde had escaped, she had a good cry of relief. Nervous that police might look for her at the train or bus station, she hitchhiked back to Dallas.

A few days later, Clyde sent a telegram from Nokomis, Illinois. He assured her that he was fine and asked her to pass along the news to his mother. He loved his girl, he told her, and would write soon.

Neither Bonnie nor Clyde dared to tell their mothers about her assistance. Both moms said they learned about her role in the escape only years later. But for Bonnie Parker and Clyde Barrow, that day changed everything. Bonnie wasn't just Clyde's sweetheart; she was truly his partner in crime.

5

EASTHAM FARM, TEXAS PRISON SYSTEM, 1930–1932.—

---◇---

We each of us have a good "alibi"
For being down here in the "joint;"
But few of them really are justified
If you get right down to the point.

—Bonnie Parker, "The Story of Suicide Sal"

JUST DAYS after Lee Simmons became the manager of the Texas prison system in April 1930, he made room for Clyde Barrow and thirty-nine other new prisoners to relieve crowding in local jails.

Simmons, a fifty-six-year-old former sheriff and businessman, pledged to clean up the prison system, which had been plagued by overcrowding, prisoner escapes, and high costs.

Amid charges that prisoners were mistreated and beaten, he promised to forbid guards from cursing at inmates or whipping them at will in the fields.

"From this time on," he said, "every prisoner is some mother's son, some woman's husband, some sister's brother. I expect you to treat them as human beings."

He opposed putting prisoners in solitary confinement, calling it "inhuman." Instead, he believed all prisoners should work rather than sit in a cell, both for their own health and also for the benefit of the system, which ran eleven farms that brought in money for the state.

Above: Texas prison manager Lee Simmons, in the 1930s.

Right: The leather "bat" used to whip prisoners.

His pledges made for good newspaper copy. But in truth, as Clyde would soon learn, the prison system remained as brutal as ever, especially for the poor whites, blacks, and Latinos who often got long sentences. There was little leniency; prisons were for punishment, not rehabilitation.

Simmons was a vocal fan of the "bat," a two-and-a-half-inch-wide, two-foot-long leather strap that was oiled and used to flog the bare backs and buttocks of prisoners who misbehaved. The law allowed guards to get permission to administer up to twenty lashings at a time. Simmons once defended the approved whippings to legislators. "Gentlemen, it's just like using spurs" on an old horse, he told them. "When you've got your spurs on, the old horse will do the job."

From Waco, Clyde was first taken to Huntsville, the

main prison. Records from Clyde's initial physical listed him as five feet five and a half inches tall, weighing a scrawny one hundred and twenty-seven pounds. He had brown hair and brown eyes and a few tattoos, including the initials EBW with a heart and dagger on his left forearm, a US Navy tattoo (though he was never in the navy), and an image of a girl's face on his right forearm (another former girlfriend).

He showed some pluck in listing his personal information. Instead of Clyde Chestnut Barrow, he gave his middle name as Champion. He listed his age as eighteen. And he wrote that Bonnie Parker was his wife, because inmates could receive mail only from relatives, not from girlfriends.

During the summer, Clyde spent some time in jails around the state, facing additional charges, but they were all dropped for lack of evidence. His last stop was back in Waco, where he learned he would be assigned to the Eastham Farm.

On the bus ride back to prison, he met Ralph Fults, an Eastham escapee who was being returned. Clyde asked him what the farm was like.

Fults painted a frightful picture. If you didn't obey the guards, "they'll bust your head open," his new friend said.

The guards would kill, Fults warned, for two things: escaping and not working quickly enough. For the first escape, a convict could expect a severe beating. The second time, Fults said, "they take you over some hill and put a slug in the back of your head. 'Attempted escape,' they call it. We call it 'spot killing.'"

Clyde saw the treatment firsthand not long after he and Fults were assigned to Camp 2 at Eastham. While the two friends were working together on a woodpile, three guards surrounded Fults and beat him with the butt of a pistol until his head was bloody and his eyes were swollen shut. At some risk to his own safety, Barrow stayed close by, watching, and drawing the attention of other guards who had surrounded them. When the beating was over, he helped Fults up.

Years later, Fults told writer John Neal Phillips that he believed Barrow's willingness to be a witness saved his life. It also earned him Fults's unending loyalty—and lit an angry fire in Barrow that simmered for years. "They ain't supposed to be doing that kind of thing," Barrow told Fults later that night. "It's just not right."

Right then, Barrow began hatching plots to get revenge once he was free again.

But he first had to survive the brutal life of an Eastham prisoner. Under Simmons's leadership, the workday grew to ten hours from nine. In reality, it may have been longer: Barrow and Fults joked about their "eight hour days," which ran from eight in the morning until eight at night. Inmates were expected to run in a single-file line at full speed about two miles to the farm, and to run back after the long day in the fields. Those who couldn't keep up were beaten.

Lunch was a five- to ten-minute break for cornbread and water. Dinner wasn't much better. Food vendors often dumped their spoiled goods on the prison; much of the other food came out of a can.

Huntsville and the prison farms lacked proper sewer systems. "Everywhere was filth and garbage," Simmons said.

In his autobiography, Simmons said he worked to clean up the conditions and started a garden for fresh food. But he also pushed the farms to produce more and work inmates harder so the state wouldn't lose money. And though he told news reporters otherwise, the way guards treated prisoners didn't change. One punishment required handcuffed prisoners to stand on a vinegar barrel for hours on end—sometimes all night, even as their legs went numb. If they fell off, they would be hoisted up again and again.

Records from just six months in 1931 showed that 128 people were officially flogged—and many more were beaten unofficially. One fellow Eastham inmate said later that he had seen guards kill five prisoners during his time there.

Nell Barrow Cowan, Clyde's sister, remembered one visit where both her brother's eyes were black and blue. Later, he told her he had been beaten for not keeping up in the fields. Another time, he said he was beaten for allegedly passing a note to her.

Through much of this, Fults remembered, Barrow still joked around and "loved to laugh." Fults found him generally quiet

Clyde's Texas prison record.

and reflective, though he fumed over the injustice of prison life. "He couldn't stand to see those guys getting beat up all the time," Fults remembered. "He got real bitter." Clyde could also be moody and quick to explode in anger.

Clyde was close to his family, and spoke to Fults regularly about his mother and his brother Buck. (Buck had entered prison in January 1930. About two months later, he simply walked out, stole a car, and headed to Dallas. While Clyde was serving his sentence, Buck was spending a lot of time at home.)

Clyde also told Fults about Bonnie, his "little blue-eyed girl," and how much he loved her. Clyde's long absence was hard on Bonnie. She didn't visit, but Fults remembered Clyde receiving letters from her.

The bond that Fults and Barrow built in that grim camp was severed after some months, when Clyde was removed from the fields one day and relocated to Eastham's Camp 1. Guards apparently were worried about the friendship between the Dallas man and the one-time escapee.

In Camp 1, Clyde encountered a new kind of abuse. Within the walls, administrators relied on prisoners known as building tenders and trustys to help keep order among all the inmates. These building tenders and trustys were often prisoners facing long sentences who were unofficial enforcers, contributing to the violence. They held down prisoners as they were whipped with the bat, and often, they thrashed fellow inmates themselves, without facing penalties.

Camp 1 had a particularly vicious building tender named Ed Crowder. By some accounts, Crowder was a big man, more than six feet tall, though his prison papers listed him as five feet eight inches. He singled out Clyde for harsh treatment and, according to Fults, sexually assaulted him. Like many building tenders, he had a number of enemies.

In late October 1931, newspapers reported that Crowder, serving time for bank robbery, had been killed in a knife fight with Aubrey Scalley, who was serving a fifty-year sentence for multiple robberies.

But others said it was Clyde who couldn't take the abuse anymore. Clyde hatched a plan with Scalley, who also despised Crowder. Clyde would handle the killing and Scalley would take the blame for it, since he already had a long prison term.

Late one evening, Clyde headed to the toilet, a piece of pipe concealed in his trousers. Crowder, seeing his victim alone, followed.

When his tormenter approached, Clyde hit him in the head with the pipe. Crowder collapsed.

Scalley stepped in, cutting himself superficially with a knife and then stabbing Crowder, who was already fatally wounded.

Though Scalley won some time in solitary confinement, there was no real investigation. Prison officials knew Clyde and Scalley had worked together. But Clyde apparently wasn't punished for committing his first murder.

———•———

Back in West Dallas, Clyde's parents had been doing slightly better financially. One of the older kids had bought a piece of land on nearby Eagle Ford Road, and Henry and Cumie loaded their small, hand-built house onto a truck and moved it to the new lot. There, Henry made the front room a filling station, selling gas, sodas, and other small items. Some say he sold bootleg liquor from under the counter during Prohibition. He had the only water well in the area and sold fresh water to the locals, sometimes trading for produce or other goods instead of cash.

The rest of the home was spare, without electricity or insulation; plumbing consisted of an outhouse in the back. The family was barely squeaking by. But that was better than before—and better than many Americans were doing. The Great Depression was devouring the nation, and more and more people were losing both their jobs and their homes. The old campground where the Barrows had first lived was now more crowded than ever with people who had lost everything.

Cumie, though, had another source of cash: Buck had been actively robbing businesses. The money was used to hire lawyers to work on Clyde's behalf.

In November 1931, shortly after Crowder's murder, Dallas lawyers working for the Barrows wrote the state's pardon board, saying Clyde had been treated unfairly back in 1930. The family of one of his Waco accomplices had been able to hire a lawyer to appeal their son's sentence; on appeal, that longer sentence was cut back. But at the time, Clyde couldn't afford a lawyer, which his lawyers now claimed was an injustice. They also told a fib about Clyde's parents to make him seem more sympathetic. "Therefore, we ask you to recommend to our Governor to let this youth come home to his mother at Dallas, who is a widow and who is in necessitous circumstances of the earnings of her son."

In the following weeks, Clyde's lawyers were able to drum up additional support. A Waco district attorney added his own letter to the file, saying that Clyde "was a young fellow of nice appearance, has plenty of sense to make a good citizen." Another letter, signed by Judge Munroe along with the former McLennan County sheriff and others, also supported his parole, saying his mother needed help.

On January 7, the state pardon board asked Governor Ross Sterling to consider his release. "In view of the fact Barrow was only 18 years old when he got into his trouble, because he pleaded guilty, because he has served two years and four months, because he has been recommended by all of the trial officers, it is the opinion of the pardon board that he may be appropriately given a parole for the rest of his term, conditioned upon his good behavior and his going to the care and support of his mother," the pardon board wrote.

Things were looking up for Clyde—but he didn't know it. Cumie had been telling him for more than a year that she was working to get him released. But as months passed and nothing happened, he grew increasingly despondent.

Eastham was wearing him down. The endless, backbreaking work. The whippings and the punishments. The long stretches without seeing family. Over the years, dozens of Eastham prisoners, suffering from exhaustion and mistreatment, cut their own Achilles tendons to get a break from the fields. Others broke bones in their feet or convinced a fellow convict to take the drastic measure of cutting off some of their fingers or toes.

When the self-mutilation made Texas newspapers, prison officials dismissed the prisoners who took such extreme actions as lazy people who simply didn't want to work.

But, said Michael Crawley, an inmate in the early 1930s, "I'm telling you that is not true." During his time, he was forced to stand on a barrel for eight nights, beaten, shot, and threatened with death. "I figured it was my life or my hand," he told a reporter. "There were many times I wanted to die, but life is sweet. So I put my hand down on a stone and cut it twice," severing his fingers.

The injuries usually put inmates in the Huntsville prison hospital, at least for a little while.

In mid-January, Clyde convinced a fellow inmate to cut off two toes on his left foot with a sharp tool.

Some family members said that Clyde couldn't take the abuse anymore. Others cited another factor: his older brother Buck had finally returned to prison after Christmas, giving in to his wife's and Cumie's pleas to finish his term rather than live as an escapee. Clyde may have been desperate to see Buck, who was serving his time in Huntsville.

Soon after his injury, he was admitted to the infirmary at Huntsville.

On January 27, Governor Sterling signed Clyde's parole papers in Austin.

Clyde learned that his sentence had been shortened just a few days before he left prison on February 2. He hobbled out on crutches, a very different man from the youngster who had entered less than two years earlier. Ralph Fults would later say that prison changed Clyde from "a schoolboy to a rattlesnake." Clyde's foot would heal, but he would remain angry and distrustful. And without much of his two biggest left toes, he would always walk with a limp.

As the lawyers and others had promised, he would help support his mother—but not in the way they expected.

6

ELECTRA, TEX., APRIL 14, 1932.—

———◦———

If he had returned to me sometime,
Though he hadn't a cent to give,
I'd forget all this hell that he's caused me,
And love him as long as I live.

—Bonnie Parker, "The Story of Suicide Sal"

SHORTLY AFTER he returned to West Dallas, Clyde Barrow cleaned up, put on fresh clothes, and went to see Bonnie Parker Thornton.

When he arrived, she was visiting with a new boyfriend. But as soon as she saw Clyde, she rushed into his arms. The new beau got the message and departed. Emma Parker's disappointment with Clyde's reappearance, however, lingered.

Bonnie's mother tried to talk some sense into Clyde, who was now in his early twenties. She urged him to get a job and stay out of trouble. But his charm was in high gear, "his dimple and smile working," she said, and he didn't want to hear it. He told her that no one was likely to hire him.

Did Clyde Barrow ever intend to lead a crime-free life after prison? Some of his family thought it was possible. He talked about repairing cars behind his father's Eagle Ford Road gas station, but he didn't do much to make that happen.

The police were watching him again, of course, and his family believed he should leave town and start over. His sister Nell lined up

The Barrow filling station in West Dallas, circa 1932.

a construction job with a friend in Massachusetts, thousands of miles from his troubles. He traveled there, but didn't stay long. The man who hired him reported Clyde was nervous and couldn't calm down and just do his job. He lasted at most two weeks before he returned home.

He told Nell that he couldn't stop thinking about his treatment at Eastham. And he missed his family terribly. "I've got to stay close to home," he said.

At some point, according to his friend Ralph Fults, Clyde returned to work at United Glass and Mirror. But as before, the police kept coming in and "draggin' me downtown," Clyde said. With so many other people out of work in the Depression, the company didn't need an ex-con who missed so much work. It let him go.

Clyde returned to the Barrow filling station fed up, his rage and bitter feelings toward authority overflowing. Fults had come over to visit, and Clyde told his mother and his friend that he was done with trying to live by the rules.

"I'm never gonna work again. And I'll never go back to that hell-hole" at Eastham, he insisted.

"They're gonna have to kill me," he went on. "I swear it, they're gonna have to kill me."

He made the promise in a moment of anger—but it was one he would keep. He never did try a regular job again. Instead, he chose to get by however he could, while also mulling over revenge on those who had treated him so badly. While they were locked up and then after they were free, Clyde talked often to Fults about returning to Eastham to lead a big prison break, payback for the cruel treatment he and other inmates had suffered.

But a jailbreak took money and weapons, and the young men didn't have either. So within days, he and Fults were back to what they knew best: crime. Despite their records, they were rusty, and it showed. Tipped off to a big payroll, they tried to rob a local oil company. But after tying up employees, they broke into the safe and found it empty.

When Clyde and Fults had been in prison, fellow inmates had schooled them in the art of bank robbing, which required research, surveillance, and careful planning for success. On the way back from a road trip to Minnesota, Clyde, Fults, and another West Dallas friend, Raymond Hamilton, tried out their lessons.

Fults said that they robbed a bank of thousands of dollars. It isn't clear where the bank was, or how much they actually got, but the unexpected ease of the robbery gave them confidence. They stopped to buy a few high-powered weapons from a dealer, including a fast-firing Thompson submachine gun, and bullet-proof vests, and they returned to West Dallas with a cache of cash and guns.

Back home, they glumly discovered their purchases were less than perfect. Gathering with friends at a lake between Dallas and Denton, Barrow and Fults put the vests to the test; they fell apart under fire. The guns were balky and seemingly defective.

Hanging on to money was also a challenge. Clyde went through much of his share quickly, giving it to relatives and friends in West Dallas. Such generosity wasn't just from the heart: his money helped needy loved ones, true, but it also bought him much-needed loyalty and protection. When police came around to ask questions, his neighbors wouldn't have any answers.

Clyde still had some money left for an Eastham raid. But he wanted more men and more weapons. In mid-April, he, Fults, and a third young man headed to the Texas panhandle to look up some former inmate acquaintances to join their effort. Unsuccessful in their search, they were on their way back when their car broke down in Electra, Texas, a town near the Oklahoma border.

Three unknown young men strolling toward the center of town was a bad sign, especially because the famous Oklahoma bank robber, Charles "Pretty Boy" Floyd, had supposedly been spotted there recently. A local businessman alerted the police.

Police Chief James T. Taylor drove up with another city official. Clyde and Fults's friend sensed big trouble and ran off.

Chief Taylor said that the young men pulled guns on them right away.

But Fults, in an interview years later, said the chief had pulled out handcuffs and told Clyde and him, "I gotta take you down."

To avoid arrest, Fults pulled a gun from his shirt and shoved it into the chief's face, which allowed him to take the chief's gun. Clyde pointed his weapon at the other city official.

While they had their guns on the two Electra officials, Clyde and Fults were suddenly joined by the businessman A. F. McCormick, who had first spotted them. They forced all three into McCormick's car at gunpoint, and Clyde, sporting large tortoiseshell sunglasses, took the wheel. The kidnappers told their hostages that they were taking a ride because "they could not afford to go to jail."

About ten miles out of town, Clyde and Fults dropped the Electra men off near a local ranch, promising to take good care of the car and the chief's gun.

Their getaway car ran out of gas a few miles down the road and Clyde and Fults pulled their guns on the first driver they saw, mail carrier W. N. Owens. Clyde drove Fults and Owens along dirt roads around Wichita Falls and into Oklahoma. Unable to pay the bridge toll at the state border, Clyde busted through a chain gate. The toll-takers shot at them, but didn't hit anything.

Along the way, Clyde and Fults took the eight cents in Owens's wallet and traded some of his postage stamps for gasoline. By then, they were all famished. The young men told the mailman that they hadn't eaten in three days. Finally, they were able to convince a lunch stand operator to give them some food, which they shared with Owens. About one hundred miles from Electra, they left Owens on the side of the road, his mailbags next to him, and then wound their way back toward home.

Later, people looking for folk heroes in the depths of the Depression would see Clyde's willingness to let these hostages and others go unharmed as a sign that he had a soft-hearted side and he wasn't the evil, cold-blooded murderer that law-enforcement described. But letting people go unharmed didn't mean he didn't first scare them half to death. Owens was terrified Fults was going to kill him, and the local newspaper reported that "Mrs. Owens was frantic with grief" over his disappearance.

———◦———

Back in Denton, Clyde and Fults regrouped with their friends to work on the details of a prison break. On April 17, they picked up Bonnie from her mother's house and headed south toward the Eastham Farm. Bonnie went in alone, telling guards she was Aubrey Scalley's cousin; she told Scalley that Clyde would try to bust him out soon.

The road trip was Fults's first chance to spend time with Bonnie and he liked her right away. She was "bright, refreshing, and pleasant to be with," he said later. She was working again and was a popular waitress. He found her friendly and chatty, and hardly cut out for a life of crime.

But she didn't see a hopeful future for herself. "I'm just a loser—like Clyde," she told Fults. "Folks like us haven't got a chance."

The next night, the trio headed to East Texas to steal cars that would be big enough to transport several freed prisoners. On the way, they stopped in Kaufman to buy some ammunition at a local store and admired the weapons on display.

After taking two big cars, a Buick and a Chrysler, Clyde and Fults decided to relieve the store in Kaufman of some of its guns. It was an unusually poor decision, even for them.

A night watchman spotted them and approached. Clyde shot

at him and the watchman returned fire. He also sounded the town alarm, a fire bell. Alert townspeople responded quickly.

Clyde and Bonnie jumped into one car and Fults in the other, but the first road they approached was blocked with construction equipment. They circled back through the square and then had to circle back again when a second road appeared to be blocked, too. Finally, they found a narrow road out.

Then, the sky opened up. Water came down in sheets—a true April deluge. The road grew soggy and then swampy. Before long, both cars had settled deep into East Texas mud.

Clyde ran to a nearby farmhouse. Unable to find a car, he stole two mules.

With drizzle still coming down, Clyde and Bonnie got on one mule and Fults on the other, and they trudged through most of the wet night in hopes of finding another car and a safe ending to a disastrous outing. Near dawn, they spotted a car at a farmhouse and traded their mules for a better ride. They didn't get far, however, before that car ran out of gas.

Almost all day, the trio hid from bands of searchers. Eventually, they were spotted and a posse descended toward them. The three dove into the brush near Cedar Creek to hide as shots rang out. By then, Bonnie had lost her shoes and her dress was torn. Clyde and Fults responded with fire, aiming, they said, above the searchers' heads. Fults was hit in the left arm.

Certain they were about to be captured, Clyde decided to make a run for it. He told Bonnie and Fults that he would come back with help, and took off. Somehow, after so many missteps, his timing was finally right. He darted between two men just as they were reloading their guns.

At Fults's urging, Bonnie gave herself up. Fults was captured a few minutes later.

The two were taken to Kemp, Texas's tiny calaboose, a small brick building with a dirt floor that seemed more like an outhouse than a jail. For the first couple of hours, Bonnie stood by the iron grate door, demanding that the townspeople staring at them get Fults medical treatment for his injured arm. Her requests were ignored. The last car they had stolen, it turned out, belonged to the town doctor, who hadn't been the least bit happy to wake up to two mules outside his home. He refused to help.

The pair spent the night on display as folks gawked at them and armed locals stood on guard.

The next day, April 20, they were taken to the bigger Kaufman County jail, where Fults's arm was finally treated. Neither he nor Bonnie would identify their missing accomplice.

The Kemp calaboose, in a recent photo.

Within a week, Fults had been linked to the Electra kidnappings and was transferred to Wichita Falls. He was quickly tried and sentenced to more than ten years in prison.

Bonnie Thornton, the married name that the newspapers used, was left in the Kaufman County jail until a grand jury could meet to decide if she would be charged with a crime. The jailer and his wife were kind to her and let her play with their children and sit outside in the evenings. Clyde's younger brother L. C. and his brother Buck's wife, Blanche, checked on Bonnie occasionally, and, at Clyde's urging, Cumie Barrow sent a new dress and bought Bonnie some new shoes.

Emma Parker visited, too, though seeing her precious daughter in jail was wrenching to her. "All in all, it was enough to break a mother's heart," Bonnie's mother said, "but I was to learn later that the human heart can stand many, many breakings and still keep right on beating."

Emma wanted to bail Bonnie out, but she didn't have the money to do it. Nor was there money for a lawyer. The jailer's wife urged Emma to wait, saying that Bonnie wasn't likely to be charged with a crime and a jail stay might ultimately be good for her.

To pass the time, Bonnie worked on at least one poem, which she titled "The Story of Suicide Sal." The verse, reflecting her love of drama and storytelling, was a long rhyming narrative about an outlaw's girlfriend named Sal, who ends up in jail. (Later, after copies of the poem were found, Bonnie's use of gangster terms, like *hot*, to mean someone who is wanted, and *hotsquat* for the electric chair, led some to believe she was already a true outlaw herself. But it is also possible that as an avid reader, she'd picked up the vocabulary from newspapers, true detective magazines, and dime-store novels.)

In the story, the former boyfriend takes up with a new woman rather than waiting for Sal. Angered, Sal tracks down the couple once she is out. She seeks revenge—and then is murdered herself, apparently by machine-gun wielding gangsters.

Not long ago I read in the paper

That a gal on the East Side got "hot,"

And when the smoke finally retreated,

Two of gangdom were found "on the spot."

It related the colorful story

Of a "jilted gangster gal."

Two days later, a "sub-gun" ended

The story of "Suicide Sal."

———

While Bonnie and Fults languished in jail, Clyde returned quickly to the business of crime. The same day his friends were transferred to the Kaufman jail, Clyde and some of his other pals robbed a hardware store of rifles and shotguns. On April 30, he and one or two Denton friends checked out a combination filling station and jewelry store in Hillsboro, Texas, south of Dallas.

After casing the place, Clyde and his Denton pals made plans to rob the store late that night. Some believe Clyde was one of the men who went in the store. But Clyde's family insisted that he stayed in the car as the getaway driver.

What is certain is that someone banged on the door and

called for owner John Bucher by name, asking to buy guitar strings. Two men entered. They wanted to pay for the strings with a ten-dollar bill, requiring Bucher to open the safe to make change.

Bucher called his wife, Madora, to help him with the combination. Then, sensing trouble, he reached for his gun. One of the robbers fired first, hitting the man in the chest. Bucher died that night.

The thieves left with $40, about $2,500 worth of diamond rings, and Bucher's gun.

Authorities believed Clyde and his old friend Frank Clause were responsible for the murder of John Bucher, as shown in this wanted notice from Hill County. Later, Madora Bucher would identify Raymond Hamilton as Clyde's accomplice.

Clyde's big plans were not going well. Bonnie and Fults were locked up, and he had just participated in a senseless murder. An Eastham prison break would have to wait.

JOHN N. BUCHER, 1871–1932

John N. Bucher was sixty-one years old and a prominent, long-time Hillsboro resident when he was gunned down at his store.

Born in Arkansas, he moved to Texas at age eighteen and settled in Hillsboro in the late 1890s. He rented and repaired bicycles and then became one of the town's first automobile owners.

As cars grew more popular, Bucher became an expert auto

John N. Bucher, Hillsboro, Texas, store owner.

mechanic. He also made eyeglasses and had a special talent for designing fine jewelry. His combination filling station and store was eclectic, carrying bicycles, knickknacks, and used watches. He and his second wife, Madora, lived upstairs. Given the times, he may also have been operating as a pawnshop.

Bucher was widowed in 1902 and married Madora a few years later. His survivors included a son from his first marriage, his wife, and two sons and two daughters from his second marriage, three of whom were developmentally disabled.

7

STRINGTOWN, OKLA., AUGUST 5, 1932.—

---○---

Now Bonnie and Clyde are the Barrow gang.
I'm sure you all have read
    How they rob and steal
    And how those who squeal
Are usually found dying or dead.

—Bonnie Parker, "The Story of Bonnie and Clyde"

CLYDE BARROW was getting quite a bad reputation in some of the smaller towns in Texas.

In mid-May 1932, as Bonnie waited in the Kaufman County jail, the *Electra News* reported that the police chief there had identified Clyde as his other kidnapper from a mug shot. Mail carrier Owens described tattoos that matched Clyde's.

And, the paper said, he was also wanted for John Bucher's cold-blooded murder, suggesting that Clyde was actually in the store. The Texas governor was offering a $250 reward to help find the dangerous thieves who had killed the storekeeper.

In mid-June, the grand jury in Kaufman finally met to decide Bonnie's fate. Bonnie testified that she didn't know the men she was with. Charges were dropped and she was released.

Back home, Emma Parker found her middle child more sober, "more quiet, and a great deal older" than the twenty-one-year-old who had left home in April.

Her mother warned her that Clyde was heading down a dangerous path and Bonnie should keep her distance. "I'm through with him," Bonnie told her with a serious face. "I'm never going to have anything more to do with him."

Perhaps Bonnie didn't

Bonnie and her mother, Emma Parker, at a family gathering, 1933.

want to hurt her mother. Or maybe she just didn't want to argue with a woman who was as strong-willed as she was. But she was lying through her teeth.

In late June, she told her family she had a job prospect in Wichita Falls and left town.

In truth, she was joining Clyde, who had rented a little place there to get out of Dallas. Over the next two years, the couple would regularly take refuge in such hideouts for a few days up to a few weeks. They were usually unknown in the area, but sometimes they were protected by relatives, fellow outlaws, or locals desperate enough for extra cash during the Depression to keep quiet about the new folks in town.

Away from the main roads, Clyde would study up on his trade. Though he lacked education, he could be a hard worker. Now his job was staying out of prison—and that wasn't easy for a career criminal to do.

Relying on fold-out maps from gas stations, he learned his way around Texas, as well as Oklahoma, Arkansas, Kansas, Missouri, and other states, creating road maps in his head. He practiced driving, especially coaxing unusually high speeds out of a variety of car models. He perfected whip-fast U-turns that allowed him to avoid roadblocks and evade pursuing police.

"He drove like a devil, and he had the luck of one," Emma Parker said.

Though he had some experience shooting guns growing up, he worked on mastering more advanced weapons. In time, his favorite weapon became the Browning automatic rifle, or B.A.R., a weapon designed for World War I that weighed about sixteen pounds. As an automatic, the B.A.R. seemed to literally shoot fire, dispensing a magazine of twenty bullets in seconds with a single pull of the trigger. The gun had a stiff recoil that could knock a slight fellow like Clyde off balance until he was accomplished with it.

Later, law enforcement officers stumbled on likely hideouts of Clyde's, including one on a hilly strip just outside of Wichita Falls. There, they discovered something of a shooting range: "There were numerous bullet holes in [the] fender of an automobile that had been used as a target, and any number of bottles had been broken, together with holes in cans, which also probably had been used as targets," a US Bureau of Investigation report said.

Today, well-trained police with modern technology and communications would have an upper hand against young guys like Clyde Barrow. But not in the early 1930s. With money tight everywhere, most departments were severely under-staffed and poorly trained. In the late 1920s, the Dallas police force numbered 328; by the early 1930s, it had dropped to 265 and then it fell some more. Pay was modest. The Dallas County sheriff's office, which monitored unincorporated West Dallas, was worse off.

Depression-era police had their hands full: the explosion in the number of cars on the road meant traffic was at least as big a headache as crime. Without safety features like seat belts, almost 32,000 people died nationwide in traffic accidents in 1931. In Dallas alone, thousands were injured each year. Pro-hibition would last until late 1933, requiring officers to deal regularly with illegal bootleggers and speakeasies.

There were no formal requirements yet to become a Dallas officer and no real training. Instead, wrote one Dallas police department historian, "The chief just stood up and asked the applicant if he knew the difference between right and wrong. If he answered yes, he was handed a badge and sent to work." Officers shot first and asked questions later.

With manpower so short, neither the city police nor the county sheriff's department had the ability to stake out a house or track a suspect. In fact, though Clyde was wanted for the Bucher murder, deputy sheriffs visited the Barrow filling station only once that summer.

Crime investigation was still in its infancy. Fingerprints lifted from crime scenes were sent for identification to the US

Bureau of Investigation, which became the Federal Bureau of Investigation in 1935. They could take weeks to get back. In early 1932, as Clyde was ratcheting up his robbery career, the Dallas police department sent an officer to Chicago for training in fingerprint identification, the origin of bloodstains, and ballistics, or the analysis of bullets and firearms. It would take time to add that expertise to the department, so most crime cases relied on eyewitness accounts, which are rarely precise.

The big news for Dallas police was the purchase of a shortwave radio system. In late 1931, the police department built a small radio station in its downtown headquarters that allowed it to broadcast bulletins to fifteen patrol cars in the field, though the officers couldn't respond. The sheriff's department soon asked for its own radio.

The system was still primitive. Because the microphone was in the middle of the office, policemen sometimes accidentally broadcast jokes and private conversations. Tuning in to KVP to hear police calls became an inexpensive hobby for locals—and local criminals. As the police would soon learn, one such shortwave radio was in regular use at the Barrow filling station.

————— o —————

During July 1932, Clyde and Bonnie shared their Wichita Falls place with Raymond Hamilton, who had joined Clyde and Ralph Fults in robberies in late March and early April. Just barely nineteen, Raymond had lived with his family for a time in West Dallas. His brother, Floyd, was a year or so older than Clyde, and one of his sisters was good friends with Clyde's little sister, Marie.

After Raymond briefly teamed up with Clyde and Fults, he had gone to Michigan to work alongside his father. He returned to Texas to learn that he and Clyde had been accused of the Bucher murder. Clyde told his family that Raymond, who was as small as Clyde, wasn't in Hillsboro that night; however, one of Clyde's accomplices looked enough like Raymond that Madora Bucher identified him from a mug shot.

During the steaming Texas summer of 1932, Clyde and Raymond paired up again. On a Monday in early August, Clyde dropped Bonnie off at the Barrow gas station, where she and Clyde stopped by almost daily to say hello. "Listen over the radio, honey," he told her, "and see if we make our getaway."

Clyde, Raymond, and an accomplice traveled a couple of miles to the Neuhoff Brothers Packing Company to try to steal the company's payroll. The men timed the crime just right: cash was being counted when they walked in a little before 5 P.M. One of them demanded, "Where is that money?"

While one held a gun on the office workers, the other plucked $440 in cash (about

Clyde (left) and Raymond Hamilton, date unknown.

$8,000 today) from a table and dropped it in a bag.

They ripped both of Neuhoff's telephones from the walls before leaving. Rushing off in a stolen auto, the thieves whipped past two cars of police officers heading to the river bottoms for target practice with an assortment of shotguns, machine guns, and pistols.

A police car tried to chase the speeders, but it was left in the dust.

Clyde picked up Bonnie, and they hurried out of West Dallas, likely using a western route known as the Devil's Back Porch. From there, they headed to an abandoned farmhouse, where they would spend the rest of the week.

On Friday, August 5, the guys decided to take a short road trip. Bonnie went to her mother's house and the men headed toward Oklahoma.

Emma Parker was overjoyed to see Bonnie for the first time in a month and they spent the evening chatting and catching up. Bonnie told her mom that she was working hard at a Wichita Falls café. Emma thought she looked tired and was more nervous than usual. Late that evening, as they sat on the porch enjoying a break from the summer heat, Emma asked Bonnie if she had seen Clyde.

"I haven't seen him and I don't want to see him," Bonnie told her, working to keep up the lie she had started earlier in the summer. Her mother would soon learn otherwise. But that night, Emma said, "I wanted to believe her more than anything in the world."

While Emma and Bonnie visited, Clyde, Raymond Hamilton, Ross Dyer, and possibly one other man—accounts differ—had crossed into southeast Oklahoma in a stolen car and spotted an outdoor dance near Stringtown. A band was playing, the crowd was growing, and Dyer wanted to stop and take a spin or two.

Though Clyde rarely drank, preferring to remain clear-headed, he and his friends were probably enjoying some bootleg whiskey that night. Dyer joined the dance, while Clyde and Raymond mostly stayed by the car, parked behind the band.

Atoka County sheriff Charles Maxwell and undersheriff Eugene Moore stopped by, in part because the sheriff wanted a ride in Moore's brand-new Chevrolet. At some point, Sheriff Maxwell noticed the outsiders Clyde and Raymond and headed over to see what they were up to. Some say he saw them drinking.

Either way, he approached them with a warning: "Consider yourselves under arrest."

He had barely gotten the words out when Clyde and Raymond both opened fire. Maxwell was struck six times before he fell, hit in the chest, arm, leg, wrist, and side. Though badly injured, he was still alive and managed to get off some shots himself. Moore came to his aid and was shot once in the chest, dying on the spot.

As the sound of gunfire rang out over the music, partygoers screamed and ran. Lights exploded from whizzing bullets. The band jumped from the stage to hide. Dancers ducked under tables and into bushes, calling out for friends.

Later, *True Detective Mysteries*, one of the many popular, cheap, and highly sensational magazines of the time, caffein-ated the drama: "Young women screamed and fainted at the sight of the bleeding officers. Their escorts, pale with anger and horror, were forced to stand by helplessly as the butchery went on."

Clyde and Raymond managed to speed off, and men at the dance pursued them, the magazine said. "Car lights shone like meteors as they swung in behind the fleeing desperadoes and dashed through the night at a speed so terrific that death lurked in every turn of the wheels."

None of the real news accounts, however, mentioned a serious chase. In truth, Clyde and Raymond jumped into their car and tried to speed away, but a tire caught on the edge of a ditch and the car rolled over.

In the chaos, they managed to escape on foot and steal a nearby car.

Before they got out of Oklahoma, that car lost a wheel, sending it careening to a stop. Spotting a farmhouse nearby, a barefoot Clyde banged on the door, saying they needed a car to get an injured woman to the hospital. Mamie Redden said later that Clyde "put up such a pitiful story" that her twenty-year-old son, Haskell Owens, agreed to take him in the family car.

Once Owens was behind the wheel, Clyde put a gun to his side, forcing him to head in a different direction. Seeing her son turn the wrong way, Redden said, "caused me so much worry I could just feel every hair on my head standing straight up."

After a while, that car broke down, too, and Owens managed to run off into the night. (Owens lived to age ninety-one, but after that frightening experience, his wife, Ruth, said, "he never answered the door at night.")

Clyde and Raymond stole yet another car, and somehow, before the scorching summer sun had come up, they were back near Dallas.

The next day, Clyde sent a friend to pick up Bonnie from her mother's house and together, they hit the road. By then, posses were swarming at least five southeast Oklahoma counties, using bloodhounds and volunteers to search for the unknown killers in the foothills near the Kiamichi Mountains. All they found were abandoned cars.

Law enforcement got a break on Sunday when they arrested a man who had boarded a bus toward Dallas. Though he gave another name, it was Dyer, who was also from West Dallas. Initially Dyer denied any involvement—but later, he seemed to have lots to say. By early the following week, Dallas newspapers reported police had "definite information" about who the two shooters were.

Four Dallas police detectives and two Dallas County deputy sheriffs, armed with machine guns and sawed-off shotguns, were assigned to track Clyde and Raymond.

Dyer tried to warn them that the men wouldn't be easy to catch. The pair was well armed and had vowed to shoot anyone who tried to arrest them. Clyde also had boasted that he would visit his Dallas family whenever he wanted, even if that meant using his gun to get in and out.

Clyde and Raymond had promised to "fight to the death," Dyer said. They would never surrender.

But law enforcement officials told the Dallas's *Daily Times Herald* that they expected arrests "would be accomplished before the end of the week." They would no doubt come to regret that boast.

EUGENE C. MOORE, 1901–1932, AND SHERIFF CHARLES MAXWELL

Far left: Under-sheriff Eugene Moore with his daughters a few years before he died.

Left: Sheriff Charles Maxwell, circa 1930.

Eugene Moore, just thirty-one when he died, was the husband of Minnie and the father of three small children: an infant boy and two daughters, ages seven and three.

Moore's father had once been a prosperous rancher and farmer but had lost it all during the Depression. So Moore became an undersheriff to feed his family. He was remembered as a man who was well liked and widely respected.

Moore's son, Russell, said later that his family moved in with his mother's parents after his dad died. She got a job, but making ends meet was difficult.

Still, he said, "the roughest thing for me was growing up without a father."

Sheriff Charles Maxwell slowly recovered from his wounds, though he was left disabled. His granddaughter recalled that, years later, a bullet remained visible in his thigh.

8

CARLSBAD, N.MEX., AUGUST 14, 1932.—

There's lots of untruths to these write-ups;

They're not so ruthless as that;

Their nature is raw;

They hate all the law—

The stool pigeons, spotters, and rats.

—Bonnie Parker, "The Story of Bonnie and Clyde"

BONNIE SUGGESTED they head to New Mexico.

In 1932, local police couldn't pursue criminals—even suspected murderers—across city, county, or state lines, though that would change in a few years. Maybe Clyde and Raymond could cool off west of Texas.

Clyde, Bonnie, and Raymond went to visit Nellie Parker Stamps, Bonnie's aunt on her father's side, near Carlsbad, New Mexico, about five hundred miles from Dallas. Initially, Aunt Nellie was happy to reunite with her niece, whom she hadn't seen in many years.

She was less sure about the two fellows with Bonnie, who were introduced to her as Bonnie's husband, "James White," and their friend "Jack Smith." The young men seemed to have an unusual amount of cash with them, and they were driving a fancy new Ford V-8 Coupe that no country person could afford.

Worried, Aunt Nellie let the local sheriff's office know of her concern.

On a Sunday morning in mid-August, Deputy Sheriff Joe Johns knocked on the door of the farmhouse. Bonnie answered.

"Whose Ford is this?" Johns asked.

Bonnie told him it belonged to the men, who were getting dressed. She promised they would be out in a minute.

Inside the house, Clyde and Raymond began to scramble. *Getting dressed* was code for trouble outside. But there was trouble inside, too: their guns were locked in the car so they wouldn't scare Nellie and her husband, Melvin, and they couldn't get to them. Finally, they discovered a shotgun in a closet and, snatching what they could of their valuables, exited from the back of the house.

Johns was studying their car with his back to the men. Clyde and Raymond snuck up on him and, with the shotgun readied, ordered Johns to get his hands up. The sheriff didn't dare reach for his own gun, especially after one of his attackers fired a warning shot into the ground.

The men ordered the sheriff into the car, and Clyde, Raymond, and Bonnie joined him. Aunt Nellie dropped to her knees, begging them not to hurt the deputy. "They told her to shut up," Johns said later, "but they did say they wouldn't hurt me."

Then, without so much as a wave good-bye, they tore down the road.

The sudden kidnapping sent the region into a frenzy. A

desperate search was launched for Johns with fifty officers from five New Mexico and Texas counties. An airplane scanned the landscape from above. Worried that the kidnappers were headed to Mexico, another two hundred and fifty men joined in to help law enforcement.

The fears grew more urgent when word got around that the deputy might have been grotesquely murdered. The shotgun warning blast had apparently blown Johns's hat off. But when the tale was repeated, it was said Johns's *head* had been shot off. That version of the rumor caught fire.

Later that day, a dead man was discovered ninety miles northeast of El Paso, Texas, and several newspapers ran frightening headlines saying the deputy had been found decapitated. The victim turned out to be someone else.

In fact, Johns was on the wildest ride of his life to the central part of Texas. Clyde sped along the muddy, unpaved roads at sixty miles an hour or more, weaving around traffic and knocking off more than one bumper as he swerved around cars.

Johns was nervous that any officers looking for them might open fire on all of them. So the deputy directed his driver through map-dot West Texas towns like Kermit, Monahans, and Crane to avoid bigger metropolises like Odessa.

During the day, it rained heavily, turning the roads into a slippery, mucky mess. At one point, Johns said, the car hit a huge wet pothole, spraying a thick layer of goo on the windshield. Rather than stop, Clyde opened his door and leaned out, still keeping his foot firmly on the gas as he pushed the speed to seventy miles an hour.

During the ordeal, the kidnappers patched several flat tires,

LEGEND HAS IT: THE FORD V-8

The Ford V-8, introduced on March 31, 1932, was a revolutionary car.

Previously, only really expensive automobiles had the zippy eight-cylinder engines. But under the careful eye of Henry Ford, engineers developed a cheaper version that could be made as a single block instead of in two pieces.

Ford introduced more than a dozen models, including two-door, four-door, and convertible options, with prices often between $500 and $600, or about $8,800 to $11,000 today.

The cars were meant to hold two passengers in the front and three in the back, though they were skinny by today's standards. A 1932 V-8 convertible sedan was six inches narrower than a 2017 Ford Fusion, making it cozy even for slender people.

Many drivers confidently left their keys in the car or failed to lock the steering column after parking, which allowed the car to be started without a key. There were door latches, too, but cars were often left unlocked.

and once left Raymond and Johns in some weeds while Clyde and Bonnie went to buy gasoline and oil. Raymond held a gun to the deputy's side during most of the trip, and from time to time, one of them would threaten to kill their hostage.

Johns feared he might die. "I wasn't nervous," he said, "but kind of half resigned to it, but with the determination that I would take every chance offered to battle them should the time actually come for the end."

Early V-8s held up to fourteen gallons of gas. But with fuel prices at 18 cents a gallon, or more than $3 a gallon in today's dollars, many Depression-era drivers put in only a little gas at a time—a likely reason Clyde often ran out of fuel. In addition, the first V-8s drank oil, wore out pistons, and broke down often.

Even paved roads of the day were rough, and flat tires were common. V-8s came with a spare tire, but drivers also could patch flat tires on the spot, inflating the repaired tire with an air pump.

The innovative and speedy Ford V-8 came in many styles, including two-door, four-door, and convertible.

While the car's average top speed was seventy-eight miles per hour, it could go ninety for several miles before the engine overheated. That was fast enough to outrun just about any other car on the road.

After the sun went down, they stopped for a break. Clyde and Raymond took a nap while the woman they called only "Honey" kept watch. At one point, she asked Johns how he liked being a criminal.

This was his first experience, Johns told her.

"You've had just 24 hours of it now," she said, "and we get 365 days of it every year."

That was a bit melodramatic. They had been on the road only

since the morning and at most, Bonnie had been on the run less than two months and Clyde only a few months longer.

Later, a rested Clyde and Raymond told Johns they had tried to quit but couldn't.

"They said the law wouldn't let them," Johns said. And they told him, "if we ever get caught, it's the electric chair for us"—his first indication that they might be experienced killers.

Finally, right before the sun came up, they stopped several miles outside of San Antonio and let Johns out. They had been on the road about twenty hours and none of them had eaten. The trio kept Johns's gun but made sure the deputy had enough money to get home. Their final words weren't exactly fond ones. "You shore have caused us a lot of trouble, sheriff," Clyde told him.

Johns replied that Clyde had caused him a little trouble, too, and "not a little worry."

His kidnapper scoffed. "You haven't been bothered much," Clyde said as he pulled away.

Johns made his way to the home of an oilman, who fed him and gave him a ride to the local sheriff's office. From there, he called his own office, reassuring the sheriff that his head was still attached and he was fine, despite "pretty rough" treatment.

Clyde, Bonnie, and Raymond continued on their endless day. Before letting Johns go, Clyde had searched for a fresh car to steal but wasn't able to find what he wanted in San Antonio.

When possible, Clyde preferred to steal Ford V-8s for their powerful flathead engine and the reinforced steel body, which could block many bullets.

That afternoon, they were more than one hundred miles to the southeast, in Victoria, Texas, when they spotted the wife of a refinery manager drive her new Ford V-8 into the garage.

Minutes later, she and her husband saw a man drive off with it. The couple alerted the sheriff's department, which soon had a report of a driver heading toward Houston, following a Ford coupe. Apparently, Clyde and Raymond figured two cars were better than one.

The sheriff's office quickly notified the nearby counties. In Wharton, roughly halfway between Victoria and Houston, officers blocked a bridge on the highway and set up an ambush. One would turn on a flashlight if he saw the cars, allowing his colleague to prepare to shoot.

As Clyde approached the bridge, he saw a light. Almost instinctively, he slammed on the brakes and turned the car around, racing in the other direction. Raymond was a little slower to respond, and by the time he had made a U-turn, bullets were flying his way. Still, both cars escaped relatively unscathed.

When they had gotten far enough away, the trio abandoned the car they had driven from Carlsbad. Raymond clambered into their newer acquisition, leaving license plates and Johns's gun behind, and the three hightailed it back to their hideout in an abandoned farmhouse west of Dallas.

On August 19, the Wharton County sheriff sent a letter to Dallas police asking for photos of Clyde C. Barrow, Raymond Hamilton, and "Bonnie Parker Alias Bonnie Thornton Alias Bonnie Smith."

"Some of our boys had a little fun with that bunch last

eveing [sic], they took two shots at one of our Deputies," the sheriff wrote. In a later letter, the sheriff accused Clyde and Raymond of trying to kill a deputy, apparently the one who had been the lookout.

Bonnie wouldn't be widely known for some months. But after participating in the New Mexico kidnapping and Wharton escape, she was quickly becoming a regular member of the Barrow gang.

LEGEND HAS IT: THE BONUS ARMY

Clyde and Bonnie's rough summer of 1932 was largely of their making. But it was a long, miserable summer as well for many others across the United States for reasons out of their control.

More than twelve million people were now unemployed, up from just one and a half million in 1929. Excluding farm workers, roughly one in three Americans who wanted to work couldn't find a paying job. Shantytowns of scrap and cardboard-box shelters sprang up on the edges of every big city, like the campgrounds in West Dallas, but much bigger.

Over the late spring and summer, an unusually large shantytown took root in Washington, DC—a camp of unemployed veterans of World War I, desperate for some help from the US government.

Calling themselves the Bonus Expeditionary Force, or the Bonus Army for short, the veterans wanted immediate payment of bonus money that they were supposed to receive in the distant future for

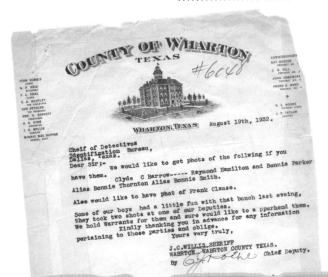

An August 19, 1932, letter from the Wharton County sheriff's office identifies Bonnie as one of the people in the car when shooting broke out a day earlier.

their service. An estimated 25,000 men, along with some women and children, set up camp in May and June in and around the capital city.

After Congress failed to reach an agreement to pay the veterans, President Herbert Hoover grew impatient. Food in the camps was in short supply and the conditions were increasingly unsanitary. On July 28, after the veterans briefly clashed with police, he ordered the military to evict the vets and their families.

General Douglas MacArthur, accompanied by Major Dwight D. Eisenhower and Major George S. Patton, guided tanks and more than two hundred troops to two camp settlements. Tear gas grenades were hurled onto the grounds, driving out occupants and setting their flimsy shelters on fire.

The cold-hearted attack on hungry, destitute men who had fought for their country would burn an ugly memory into the minds of the American public and create a stew of distrust, resentment, and anger at authority. It also made it easier for brash outlaws to seem like folk heroes to everyday people.

9

SHERMAN, TEX., OCTOBER 11, 1932.—

If a policeman is killed in Dallas,
And they have no clew or guide;
If they can't find a fiend,
They just wipe their slate clean
And hang it on Bonnie and Clyde.

—Bonnie Parker, "The Story of Bonnie and Clyde"

AFTER SO many close calls, Clyde and Bonnie needed a get-away. And according to the story their family members told, Raymond Hamilton wanted escape from the heat—both the relentless Texas sun and the relentless attention from police.

So, family members said later, Clyde and Bonnie offered to drive Raymond back to Michigan, where his father lived. After hanging out in Michigan for a little while, the couple worked their way through the Midwest.

Supposedly, they spent some fun time in Kansas City, Missouri, where Bonnie got her hair permed, and the couple was anonymous enough to go to some shows and eat out.

They traveled back to Michigan and then through Kansas and Missouri again. But they didn't return to Texas until late October, when Bonnie insisted on seeing her mother.

But the family's version isn't the whole story—and much of it probably isn't even true. Later, investigators trying to follow their trail would piece together an entirely different account of how the couple spent the fall of 1932.

Actually knowing what Clyde and Bonnie did, and when, is challenging. They didn't leave a diary, and newspaper reporters never caught up with them for interviews. They were never tried for any crimes committed after Clyde got out of prison, so no sworn testimony exists. Instead, others told their story.

In 1934, Emma Parker and Clyde's sister Nell Barrow Cowan gave their account in the book *Fugitives: The Story of Clyde Barrow and Bonnie Parker*, which included the supposed stop in Kansas City.

Jan I. Fortune, a Dallas journalist and poet, actually wrote the book, and many dates and facts are clearly wrong. After it was published, some family members criticized it as somewhat fabricated. At the same time, several of the stories matched up with various crimes. Relatives also had plenty of incentives to change certain facts or gloss over others, both to salvage what was left of Clyde's and Bonnie's reputations and also to protect themselves. Despite its significant flaws, the book is as close to a tell-all as there is.

Newspapers eager to attract readers during the Depression also chronicled Clyde and Bonnie's exploits, sometimes dramatizing the details. Inexpensive, sensationalistic detective magazines took the storytelling to new heights by, for instance, retroactively inserting Bonnie in various crimes, like the murder in Stringtown, where she wasn't present.

Victims and law enforcement shared their own versions of what happened. At times, they may have wanted to embellish their personal bravery, hide their own embarrassing missteps, or demonize the outlaws. Often, details changed when the story was repeated.

Despite the family's account of a leisurely Midwestern trip, investigators found that Clyde and Bonnie followed their disastrous visit to New Mexico with another family outing a few weeks later.

In early September, a bunch of Barrows traveled to Martinsville, a town in East Texas not far from the Louisiana border. Cumie went, along with her two youngest, L. C., who had recently turned nineteen, and Marie, now fourteen. Clyde drove them all in a Ford Coupe to see Cumie's sister Susie and her husband, Jim Muckleroy.

The visit lasted several days and was unusually uneventful except for one memorable incident: Bonnie shot herself in the foot. Literally.

Exactly why she was handling a pistol isn't known. But Muckleroy later told agents of the US Bureau of Investigation that the gun went off, striking the next-to-littlest toe on her left foot. The injury didn't appear to be serious.

After leaving the Muckleroys, Clyde and Bonnie dropped Cumie and the kids off in West Dallas and began to settle into a life on the road, with regular trips back home to see family. Using fake names, they stayed in hotels when they had the money or in tourist courts, an early version of roadside motels. Sometimes, they joined up with migrant workers traveling from farm to farm. Sometimes, the only option was to sleep in the car. Typically, they took turns sleeping so one of them could watch for any trouble.

To help pass the time, Bonnie penned poems and regularly read newspapers and detective magazines to Clyde, either buying them or stealing them from mailboxes they passed in their travels. Later, when they were better known, they especially enjoyed seeing their own names in print, even when they were accused of crimes they didn't commit.

The only money they had came from robbing small stores and filling stations and an occasional bank. They rarely had much, and cash was hard to hang on to, since living on the run was costly. Food came from cans or takeout sandwiches purchased at roadside cafés. When they could, they would drop their clothes at laundries to be cleaned and circle back days later to pick them up. Other times, they gave Clyde's family money to buy them new things to wear. In late 1932, when the US Bureau of Investigation first started to track the couple, federal agents found their trail dizzying. The new Ford V-8 stolen in Victoria, Texas—after Deputy Sheriff Johns was let go—was found around August 20 in a cornfield outside Carthage, Missouri, about seven hundred miles from where it was taken. Another car was stolen near Carthage and then dumped in early September in southern Illinois, four hundred miles away.

On September 2, a brand-new, $800 Ford Coupe was taken from a doctor's driveway in Effingham, Illinois. It was found about two weeks later near a high school in Pawhuska, Oklahoma, five hundred miles to the west of Effingham.

That last Ford offered investigators a few clues. It was left behind (and yet another was stolen) after "Mr. and Mrs. Roy Bailey"—a favorite alias of the couple—checked out of the Duncan Hotel in Pawhuska. A mix of clothing was inside, including dresses, a ladies' small slip, two pairs of men's shorts, two dress shirts, and a pair of men's pants. All of the clothes were filthy, indicating the couple might have been mostly living out of the car.

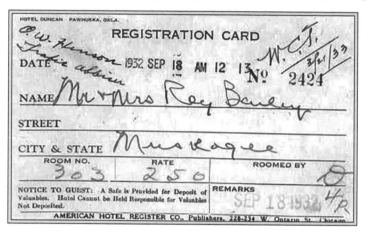

Federal agents tracking Clyde and Bonnie found this September 1932 receipt for Mr. and Mrs. Roy Bailey at a Pawhuska, Oklahoma, hotel.

The search also turned up an empty prescription bottle for Susie Muckleroy. Eventually, investigators made their way to Martinsville to interview Uncle Jim, who confirmed they had visited once. And when rumors spread that Clyde had returned or was on his way, the Muckleroy home would be raided. But the outlaws were never caught there.

As Clyde and Bonnie crisscrossed the country, they managed to stay largely under the radar until October 11. Around 6:30 P.M. that Tuesday, Howard Hall and Homer Glaze were preparing to close Little's grocery in Sherman, Texas, a town north of Dallas near the Oklahoma border, when a lone customer entered nervously. The man, wearing a tan lumber jacket and a dark hat, picked up some bread and asked a clerk for lunch meat and eggs. But as he started to pay Glaze, the man pulled out a pistol and snatched all $50 in the cash register.

"You can't do that," Hall protested. The fifty-seven-year-old butcher thought he could take on the smaller bandit and lunged at him.

The robber pushed both men toward the door, cursing and kicking at Hall. As they got close, he hit Hall hard enough to send his glasses tumbling into the street. When Hall reached for the bandit, the man fired four shots, hitting Hall three times.

Then the intruder turned the gun on Glaze, but it didn't fire.

The robber took off down the street, eventually jumping into a waiting car.

Hall was taken to a nearby hospital, where he passed away.

Glaze described the thief as a small man, about five feet six inches who was twenty to twenty-five years old, with dark hair. Dallas police sent Clyde Barrow's photo to Sherman, and Glaze quickly identified him as the attacker.

It seemed clear-cut. Clyde had a habit of robbing small stores, and the description sounded just like him. Years later, Floyd Hamilton, Raymond's older brother, said Clyde told him he had killed the butcher when he had charged him with a meat cleaver, backing him into a corner. (News accounts, however, made no mention of a knife.)

But Clyde insisted to his family that he never, ever committed a crime in Sherman. They believed him.

Why? Because "he admitted so many crimes to us, often crimes that the law knew nothing about," his sister Nell explained. "Why should he lie to us?"

That's why his family was certain someone else had pulled the trigger on John Bucher in Hillsboro while Clyde waited outside, and why they trusted that he and Bonnie were far away when Howard Hall was murdered. "We couldn't have done that," Clyde told them of the Hall murder, because they were in Kansas City at the time. "They just hung it on us for luck." And it didn't make much difference, he said, since he was already wanted for the Hillsboro and Stringtown murders.

When he and Bonnie returned to Dallas around Halloween to see their parents, they made their visit brief because a new $200 reward had been offered for Clyde's capture. Bonnie spent only long enough with her mother to give her a quick hug and kiss. And then they disappeared down the road again.

———◦———

While Clyde was building his resume as a thief and quick-trigger killer, the Dallas County sheriff was about to change. In November 1932, America elected Franklin Delano Roosevelt as its new president, and Dallas County voters elected Richard Allen Schmid, a thirty-five-year-old bicycle shop owner, as sheriff.

Known as "Smoot," a nickname from his high-school football days, Schmid was an imposing figure, standing six feet five inches tall, not counting his ten-gallon hat, with size fourteen feet. He campaigned on a promise to run an efficient, business-like department, but he had no law enforcement experience and had never handled a six-shooter before. Among his challenges was an overcrowded jail that was built for two hundred and fifty people, but often housed twice that.

When Schmid was sworn in on January 1, 1933, he replaced

Dallas sheriff Smoot Schmid with a Thompson submachine gun, date unknown.

most of the deputies. Among other things, he created a patrol division, where deputies used their own cars to patrol neighborhoods, and added uniforms, which his employees had to buy on the installment plan. (They also bought their own service weapons.)

Quickly, Schmid realized he had more to worry about than the department's finances. Despite the promise that both Dallas police and Dallas County sheriffs were on the lookout for Clyde Barrow, the elusive man remained at large. Governor Sterling had recently revoked Clyde's parole, so the outlaw would be returned to prison if he were captured alive.

Also, Clyde's former partner, Raymond Hamilton, had run out of luck. He had been arrested in Michigan a month earlier while roller-skating and then returned to Dallas. For the first time, Clyde Barrow's name appeared in the *Dallas Morning News* as Raymond's alleged partner in a number of crimes.

A Raymond Hamilton mug shot, date unknown.

Shortly after Raymond arrived in Dallas, eyewitnesses were brought in to identify him as a culprit in bank robberies, the Neuhoff holdup, and the Bucher murder. He also met the new sheriff, who found this inmate familiar looking.

"Say, don't I know you?" Schmid asked.

"You ought to," the cocky Raymond replied. "You used to buy hot bicycles from all us boys from West Dallas."

Schmid would soon be introduced to a lot more than Raymond's sass. In a matter of days, Clyde Barrow would be back in town, sorely testing the rookie sheriff's law-enforcement skills.

HOWARD HALL, 1875–1932

Howard Hall, a native of McKinney, Texas, had lived in Sherman for twenty-five years. He was married to Emma and was a father, though little is known about his family.

He had been a grocer for many years and once owned a grocery before becoming the meat-market manager at S. R. Little's store.

At his funeral, the Sherman newspaper reported, the pastor noted his courage and highlighted his "upright Christian life."

10

TEMPLE, TEX., DECEMBER 25, 1932.—

———◦———

From heart-break some people have suffered;
From weariness some people have died;
But take it all in all,
Our troubles are small
Till we get like Bonnie and Clyde.

—Bonnie Parker, "The Story of Bonnie and Clyde"

CHRISTMAS 1932 was coming and William Daniel Jones had been partying hard. Known as "Dub," "Deacon," or "W. D.," he had been out much of the evening with Clyde's younger brother L.C., working over a big bottle of homemade moonshine.

As the teenager later told police, he and L. C. ran into Clyde and Bonnie. W. D. hung out with them for a while, in part because they also had homebrew in their car. While Clyde said he still mostly avoided the stuff, Bonnie had been drinking more in response to the stress of constantly being on the run.

According to W. D., when the couple was finished visiting with family, Clyde urged him to join them on the road. They needed extra eyes to watch out for trouble, Clyde told him, while they got some sleep. W. D. said he agreed because at the time, "it

W. D. Jones, circa March 1933.

seemed sort of big to be out with two famous outlaws."

The Barrow family remembered the story very differently. W. D. idolized Clyde Barrow, said Marie, Clyde's younger sister. W. D. had an older brother, also named Clyde, who had been a good friend of Barrow's growing up, and the two families had known each other since both came to Dallas.

Like many West Dallas boys, W. D. Jones was already in the crosshairs of police, though he hadn't been in any serious trouble. (Knowing how the game was played, he claimed to be sixteen, too young to go to prison; the Barrows thought he was closer to L. C.'s age, nineteen.) To him, Clyde Barrow's life seemed like one adventure after another.

In the Barrows' telling, W. D. begged Clyde to take him along. (If Clyde really needed someone to help him, Marie said, he would have asked his brother L. C. to go along. And, in fact, L. C. did ride with Clyde sometimes.)

During the holiday visits, Clyde had shared cash and presents, giving his fourteen-year-old sister something she'd always wanted: her own bike.

But Christmas Day itself, with all its hope and celebration, turned into a dreadful one for Clyde, Bonnie, their new associate— and their victims. That afternoon, Clyde and W. D. tried to steal a new car sitting outside a home in Temple, Texas, with the keys in the ignition. As they worked to start the unfamiliar model, they caught the attention of the family gathered inside for the holiday.

Just as the engine came to life, Doyle Johnson came tearing out the front door to protect his brand-new vehicle. He jumped on the running board and grabbed for Clyde, tussling with him. W. D. stepped out of the car and pointed his weapon. Clyde's gun fired first; W. D. fired shortly after. One of the bullets hit Johnson in the neck, knocking him to the road.

Clyde and W. D. roared off. A few blocks away, they met up with Bonnie, who was waiting for them in their original car. Realizing police would soon be looking for Doyle Johnson's new car, they left it behind on the side of the road.

A mile or two away, Clyde pulled over and ordered W. D. to climb a telephone pole and cut the wires. News reports said wires were cut in nine places.

Then Clyde gave W. D. a taste of his new life: "Boy," he said, "you can't go home. You got murder on you, just like me."

Doyle Johnson, an unarmed twenty-seven-year-old husband and father, died the next day. Soon after, other Dallas men would be mistakenly accused of the crime.

That Clyde and W. D. were the killers wouldn't be known for some months. By then, they would be well into an especially murderous year.

DOYLE JOHNSON, 1905–1932

Doyle Johnson was born in Johnson County, south of Fort Worth, and moved with his family to Temple, about a hundred miles south, in 1918. According to Census records, he was a deliveryman for Strasburger's market in Temple.

He married Tilda "Tillie" Krauser when he was twenty-one and she was eighteen. The couple had been celebrating Christmas with their baby and the Krauser family when he was fatally shot.

As if he didn't have enough of his own problems, Clyde Barrow was concerned about his friend Raymond Hamilton. Raymond had been transferred to Hillsboro to be tried for John Bucher's murder, a murder Clyde insisted that Raymond didn't commit.

Nineteen-year-old Raymond was facing the possibility of the electric chair—though, in reality, few white men convicted of murder received the death penalty. Between 1930 and 1932, the state executed twenty-nine men for their crimes and more than half of them were black. Just seven were white, though whites made up the vast majority of the population. At the least, Raymond was facing a long prison sentence, and Clyde wanted to help him bust out of jail.

On the night of Friday, January 6, 1933, Clyde, Bonnie, and W. D. stopped by the West Dallas home of Raymond's older sister to touch base on their plan to get him out of jail. The older sister was out, but Maggie Fairris, a younger Hamilton sister, was there, keeping an eye on her infant boy and her sister's son.

Unexpectedly, the four-room house was full of company: two sheriff's deputies from nearby Tarrant County, an investigator for the Tarrant County district attorney, a special Texas Ranger, and a deputy sheriff from Dallas were watching from both inside and outside. By pure coincidence, the officers had chosen that night to stake out the house on the chance that a man wanted for a bank robbery would stop by.

Instead, it was Clyde who approached the front door with a sawed-off shotgun hidden under his coat. Bonnie and W. D. stayed in the car.

Unknowingly, Clyde was walking into a trap—set for some-one else. One of the deputies ordered Fairris to open the door. As she did, she told Clyde to take caution. "Oh, don't shoot!" she said. "Think of my babies."

But Clyde saw the officers in the front room and quickly took aim at them. Without hesitating, he sent a round of buckshot through the front window.

Suddenly, gunfire lit up the dark night. The other men in the house returned fire. W. D. began shooting willy-nilly from the car. Two deputies on the back porch heard the clamor and ran toward the front of the house.

As he ran around to the front porch, Tarrant County deputy sheriff Malcolm Davis saw Clyde and drew his pistol. But Clyde fired first, hitting Davis in the chest.

According to news accounts, Clyde ran for the car while W. D. provided cover. The motor was running and the three were able to race off.

None of the law enforcement officers tried to follow the shooter.

Somehow, no one else was hit during the gun battle, though windows were broken in a house down the street. Deputy Malcolm Davis, a fifty-one-year-old famous for his fresh catfish dinners, died before he got to the hospital.

MALCOLM DAVIS, 1881–1933

Deputy Sheriff Malcolm Davis.

Malcolm Davis was born in Tennessee and moved to Texas in 1893 with his father, settling in Grapevine, northeast of Fort Worth.

He had been a sheriff's deputy for several years.

A quiet, curly haired bachelor, he most enjoyed catching catfish at a local lake and inviting his friends to help eat them.

At his funeral, Reverend Frank P. Culver, Sr., presiding elder of the Fort Worth district of the Central Texas Methodist Conference, noted, "We are too ready to criticize officers of the law. We do not always realize how much their protection means. They risk their lives and too often give their lives for our peace and security."

Smoot Schmid was still barely a week into his new job as sheriff, and he was getting a painful introduction to law enforcement. He had allowed lawmen from the next county to set up a trap in his territory, but he wasn't prepared for the fallout when they were shot at by an unexpected visitor. The *Fort Worth Star-Telegram* commented that "the officers ambushed themselves."

Over the next several days, groups of heavily armed deputies and police officers patrolled Dallas, Fort Worth, and surrounding areas, and responded to an endless number of sightings from citizens looking for the unidentified shooter. Boarding houses and tourist courts were raided. Armed officers hurried to one supposed hideout after another, with no success.

More than a week later, the sheriff's office and Dallas police still weren't certain who the culprit was. The residents of West Dallas were no help. When police asked questions, friends and neighbors of the Hamiltons and Barrows had nothing to say. Some law enforcement blamed fear that Clyde might come after any snitchers.

Ted Hinton, a Dallas deputy sheriff, saw it as sign of "how Clyde had spent a fair slice of his money." Perhaps, said the *Dallas Dispatch,* Clyde and Bonnie were even "modern 'Robin Hoods,'" helping the river bottom's hungry and jobless with food and clothing. (That was probably an exaggeration, though Clyde was certainly known to leave money with family in West Dallas.)

When no new progress was made for two weeks, local newspapers sneered at the sheriff's troubles, especially when the Tarrant County sheriff suggested, without any evidence, that maybe the notorious Oklahoma bandit Pretty Boy Floyd was involved. "With Jesse James dead, and therefore practically eliminated from the search," said the *Dallas Morning News,* "peace officers turned their detective ability Thursday on another vaunted Oklahoma outlaw."

One interesting piece of information did dribble out after Raymond Hamilton was brought to the Dallas jail following an escape attempt in Hillsboro. A newspaper reported that he men-

Dallas County sheriff's deputies reenact the killing of Malcolm Davis in front of the house where he died, January 1933.

tioned a woman who was often with Clyde during his sprees—the first public hint of Bonnie Parker's involvement. According to the *Dallas Morning News*, Raymond told officers that "the girl can handle pistols with either hand as skillfully as any of the young men." W. D. later would also say Bonnie was a pretty good shot.

An officer told a reporter that he knew of such a woman. "She is as tough as the back end of a shooting gallery," he said, "and she has been missing from these parts for some time."

Emma Parker and Bonnie's brother and sister had nothing to say to the newspaper about that.

Cumie Barrow, continuing to be her son's most dedicated public defender, by contrast, spun a story of his innocence to any reporter who asked. The police might call him a cold-blooded murderer, but in Cumie's eyes, Clyde was the loving boy who dropped by around Christmas to give her a kiss and get a free fill-up at the Barrow gas station.

She admitted to being haunted by worry that he would be killed before she saw him again, adding, "We may hear any minute that he's dead."

Like a lawyer defending a criminal, she began to spell out a defense to Andrew De Shong of the *Daily Times Herald*, a few days after the shooting. "Clyde didn't kill that law the other night," she said, using a slang term for a law enforcement officer. Clyde didn't know the alleged bank robber and hadn't worked with Raymond Hamilton for months. She also told the reporter that she didn't know Bonnie, or whether she had been with Clyde.

Her son couldn't have killed John Bucher in Hillsboro because he was still on crutches at the time, Cumie insisted, and he couldn't have committed that murder in Stringtown because she saw him at 2 A.M. that night, when she fed him some leftover fried chicken.

"Has Clyde committed the murders he's accused of?" De Shong asked.

"He said he hadn't," she replied. She had asked him.

"'Son,' I said, 'did you do what they say in the papers?' and he said, 'Mother, I haven't never done anything as bad as kill a man.'"

Surely, Cumie Barrow knew better. But she loved her son, and as her daughter Nell said later, "We wanted him to live at all costs." If Cumie could cast some doubt about his guilt, maybe she could help keep him alive.

Even as Dallas and Fort Worth police chased new rumors about the outlaws' hideouts in the area, Clyde, Bonnie, and W. D. were somewhere far away. In fact, they most likely were already well outside of Texas before daylight broke after Malcolm Davis's murder.

Little was heard from them until late January, when they reemerged in Springfield, Missouri. A motorcycle officer named Thomas Persell flagged them down after seeing them circle a parked Ford. When Clyde came to a stop, Persell rode right up to the driver's door—and into Clyde's gun. "He slid the shotgun right down over the handlebars right on me and told me to get my so-and-so in the back seat, which I did," Persell said later.

Inside the car were enough guns to make a Depression-strapped police force drool, as well as sacks of what Persell was sure was money. The occupants, as a precaution, never used their real names on the road, but called themselves Bud (Clyde) and Sis (Bonnie). Bonnie had also dyed her hair red. They had some foul words for him, especially about law enforcement. "Sis" smoked all his cigarettes. "Boy"—W. D.— was mostly quiet.

When their car battery failed, they stole a new one and made Persell install it. Then, in an isolated spot near Joplin, they let him go.

Only later did he learn who his hosts had been. It had been a terrible experience, but considering their recent history, he was grateful to be alive.

LEGEND HAS IT: DID BONNIE DRIVE?

From time to time, eyewitnesses reported that a woman was behind the wheel when Clyde committed a crime. And in the murder of Malcolm Davis, *Fugitives* contends Bonnie drove around the corner and picked up Clyde, who was darting between houses.

But both Bonnie's sister, Billie, and Blanche Barrow, Clyde's sister-in-law, said they never saw her drive and didn't believe she ever learned.

11

JOPLIN, MO., APRIL 13, 1933.—

If they try to act like citizens
And rent them a nice little flat,
About the third night
They're invited to fight
By a sub gun's rat-tat-tat.

—Bonnie Parker, "The Story of Bonnie and Clyde"

CUMIE BARROW didn't just stand up for her boy Clyde. Her son Buck was still in prison, and she and Buck's wife, Blanche Caldwell Barrow, were working feverishly to legally spring him.

As they had with Clyde, they took some liberties with the facts. Blanche hitchhiked to Austin to plead for a pardon, claiming that she was expecting Buck's child. In addition, a letter from the prison's chaplain said that Buck was needed at home to support his wife, three children, and a fourth on the way.

Buck had indeed fathered three children, but one of the twin boys born to his first wife had died as an infant. He had a daughter with his second wife, but he wasn't involved in either child's life.

In truth, Blanche never had children. And she couldn't have

been carrying Buck's child since he had been in prison more than a year.

Because there was no money to hire a lawyer, Cumie tried to get a judge and prison administrators to write letters on Buck's behalf. "There were no lengths through which my mother would not have gone to help any of her kids," Marie Barrow said later.

Their persistence worked. Shortly after his thirtieth birthday in March 1933, Buck Barrow was released from prison, receiving a full pardon from Texas Governor Miriam "Ma" Ferguson only fifteen months after he'd returned to Huntsville.

Prison had made Clyde angry and bitter, but Buck said it had changed him for the better. He told Blanche and other family members that he wanted to settle down, maybe sell used cars, and stay out of trouble.

But then, he also wanted to visit with Clyde, who was six or seven years younger. He told Blanche that he was terribly worried about his kid brother and wanted to convince Clyde to turn himself in, in hopes of sparing his life.

Blanche was initially opposed to spending any time with Clyde. She sobbed. She begged Buck to stay put. She argued as best she could. But Buck was insistent.

Finally, she gave in, agreeing to join Clyde, Bonnie, and W. D. for a vacation in Joplin, Missouri. They took along her white dog, Snowball, and, as she always did, she brought her camera.

It's possible that Buck's claim that he wanted to stay out of trouble was a way of telling Blanche what she wanted to hear, much like the way Bonnie had lied to her mother about being finished with Clyde. Buck had never actually held a real job, and

Blanche and Buck Barrow, circa 1931.

she knew that, since she had accompanied him on some robberies before he went back to prison. Further, as W. D. said later, Buck had to know that he would never be able to convince Clyde to turn himself in.

On April 1, 1933, just days after Buck left prison, he and Blanche, along with Clyde, Bonnie, and W. D. moved into a Joplin apartment. Their new rental was cozy—a double garage on the first floor and two bedrooms, a kitchenette, a living room, and a small bathroom above it. It must have felt luxurious compared with prison, the Barrows' crowded home, or living on the road.

They settled in quickly. Buck and Clyde went out for quilts, bed linens, feather pillows, dishes, and silverware. Bonnie and Blanche shopped several times at a local five-and-dime, picking up scads of glassware and picture frames. Once, they splurged on twenty-cent glass rings with matching earrings. On long afternoons, Bonnie and Blanche went to the movies; occasionally, they got the guys to join them in the evenings.

For the first time in months, Clyde and Bonnie slept in real beds and ate their favorite home-cooked meals—red beans and cabbage for her and french fries and English peas with cream and a jolt of pepper for him. Buck and Bonnie also enjoyed pigs' feet and olives, while W. D. ate everything. Blanche and Clyde handled much of the cooking.

"I was glad to cook anything they wanted," Blanche wrote later, because they had so little chance to enjoy a meal when they were on the run. In particular, Clyde loved hot chocolate with lots of marshmallows. He never could seem to get enough of it.

The group stayed up playing cards until the early morning hours, while Blanche worked jigsaw puzzles; then, they all slept late the next day. They called out for groceries and laundry service. They even paid a neighborhood patrolman to keep an eye on their place.

Despite living like regular people, they were extremely cautious. Blanche or Bonnie always brought deliveries up from the first floor so the delivery boy wouldn't see the guns in the apartment. The curtains were kept closed, and they backed the car into the garage, in case they had to make a quick escape.

Though Clyde had promised to lie low during the two-week stay, he and W. D. were soon leaving during the day to rob area businesses. One day, all three men came back late at night with a huge new cache of guns, stolen from an unguarded National Guard armory. They spent the next day out in the country, testing them. As their visit stretched to two weeks, W. D. also stole another car.

Bonnie was angry that they had added another car to the mix, sure that it would bring more attention to the group. She and Clyde argued, and as happened sometimes with them, it escalated into a physical fight. "He knocked her across the bedroom a couple of times but she got up and went back for more," Blanche remembered. W. D. also witnessed Clyde hitting Bonnie, he said later, followed by Clyde trying to kiss and make up quickly.

By Thursday, April 13, they were all antsy. Blanche wanted to get on with her new life with her now-free husband. Clyde was fretting that all their activity in the area was attracting notice. They made plans to leave the next day, Good Friday, April 14, and began to pack their belongings.

Around 4 P.M., Blanche was washing some clothes in the sink and Bonnie was finishing her latest revisions on "Suicide Sal" when two Joplin police officers and two troopers from the Missouri State Police drove up in two cars.

Suspecting bootleggers or car thieves, the officers arrived with nothing more than their service revolvers and a warrant to search for liquor. With them was Wes Harryman, a father of six who was in his first term as county constable; his job was to deliver warrants.

The group saw Clyde and W. D. trying to shut the garage door. "Just a minute," one officer called out. "We want to talk to you."

Joplin detective Tom DeGraff pulled up to block the garage, and shouted to Harryman, "Get in there as quickly as you can before they close that door!"

Harryman took three steps from the car into the garage, getting off one round. He was swiftly met with a hail of No. 1 buckshot—lead balls nearly the size of a pea—that pounded into his neck and shoulder, killing him.

Harry McGinnis, a Joplin car-theft detective, squeezed off three shots as he emerged from the backseat. Then, he, too, was hit with a barrage of buckshot. His right arm was nearly severed, and he was struck in the left side and face before falling near the car.

DeGraff tried to shoot from behind the car, and then by the house. Meanwhile, the two state troopers took aim with their revolvers; one of them hit W. D. in the side.

"For God's sake," DeGraff yelled at one of the troopers, "run to that house and phone the station to send more men out here!"

Clyde shouted at Bonnie and Blanche to get in the car. Hearing the shots, Buck had run downstairs to help his brother. W. D. had stumbled up the stairs clutching his stomach, certain he was about to die. Blanche gave up on gathering her things to help him back downstairs.

For a few moments, the shooting stopped as one trooper sought more help and the other two officers pulled back to reload and reassess their situation.

The outlaws realized the police car was blocking their escape. Buck or Clyde released the brake on it, and Buck stopped to move the dead officer out of the way. In the commotion, Blanche's dog, Snowball, had run outside and she had followed him down the street, trying to find him. Somehow, the other four made it into the car, along with an armful of weapons—but not much else.

Clyde gave the police car a solid bump with their Ford, sending it down a small hill and across the street, where it hit a tree. As soon as it was gone, Clyde blasted out of the garage. He picked up Blanche a block or so away. The dog had disappeared.

The officers, outgunned and outrun, were in no position to follow or even offer parting shots. Harryman was dead, and McGinnis died a few hours later.

JOHN WESLEY HARRYMAN, 1881–1933, AND HARRY MCGINNIS, 1879–1933

Wes Harryman, Jasper County, Missouri, constable.

Wes Harryman, forty-two years old, had been a constable for only a few months when he was shot down. Like so many farmers, he couldn't make a living and had run for the office to help support his family.

In that job, he didn't get a regular salary but was paid based on the warrants he delivered and other duties.

Harryman's oldest son, Claude, was twenty at the time of his father's death and took jobs to help support his four younger siblings, including butchering animals. His mom took sewing work and they sold the farm.

"It wasn't until my brothers and sisters grew up that I could make plans, get married, settle down on my own place," he said later.

Harry McGinnis, fifty-three, had been an officer for eight years and was nicknamed "the Irishman." He was a friendly and popular policeman who had served as acting chief of detectives.

His first wife had died two years earlier after being hit by a car. He had planned to marry his fiancée in May 1933.

Harry McGinnis, Joplin, Missouri, detective.

Inside the getaway car, W. D.'s clothes and Blanche's dress were soaked with blood, and Clyde was bleeding from a wound to the chest.

In the course of a few minutes, everything had changed. Buck and Blanche, who had just celebrated a new future, would now be hunted for murder, along with Clyde and Bonnie. W. D. wasn't sure he would live through the night.

And then there was the evidence left behind. Inside Blanche's bag, police found her marriage license, her camera, and Buck's recent pardon, so there was no doubt who they were. A Wanted poster with Clyde's and Buck's photos—but not Bonnie's—was sent to police in every town of more than one thousand people in the middle of the country.

Investigators asked a local newspaper to develop the film they found. They were puzzled by the identity of the younger man; no one knew who W. D. was. But photos of Clyde and Bonnie, including the soon-to-be-famous one of Bonnie with a gun and that awful cigar, started appearing in all kinds of newspapers and magazines. They weren't just a pair of young criminals, but attractive and well-dressed ones.

All that press was more attention than the couple could have ever imagined. Soon, people across the country would know the faces of Clyde Barrow and his female partner, Bonnie Parker.

———o———

Realizing that police in several states would be looking for them, Clyde headed to West Texas and hardly paused until they got to the Texas Panhandle, about five hundred miles from Joplin. There they bought some rubbing alcohol and

Newspapers from coast to coast
published Bonnie's scandalous Joplin photo.

Mercurochrome to clean up their injuries.

Clyde covered an elm branch with gauze and poked it into
the wound in W. D.'s side. He found it was a clean shot—the
bullet had exited his back just below the ribs—so they were
confident it would heal. The bullet fragment in Clyde wasn't
very deep and Bonnie was able to pop it out with a hairpin. Buck
thought he had been hit but was only bruised.

As their photos began to make the news, police told law
enforcement from Texas to Missouri to "shoot to kill." Believing
the Barrows would make their way back to their family, Dallas
police said they were keeping some houses in West Dallas under
close watch.

Even so, D. E. Walsh, head of the Dallas police department's
identification bureau, told reporters that Cumie Barrow, ever
her family's defender, insisted that her sons had never killed

Clyde (left) and W. D. in a photo from the film left behind in Joplin.

anyone and that they were "being framed."

Walsh admitted the police knew that Clyde was regularly visiting his parents' home but hadn't been able to catch him in town.

With Missouri and Texas feeling dangerous, the next two weeks were a blur for the fugitives as they sped through state after state in the nation's midsection: Texas to New Mexico to Kansas, Nebraska, Iowa, and Illinois, where they robbed another National Guard armory. Then they went back through Missouri, Arkansas, Oklahoma, and Louisiana.

"Run, run, run. At times, that seemed all we did," W. D. said later.

More often than not, they slept in the car or outdoors. As he always did, when Clyde thought everyone else was asleep, he got on his knees and prayed. At the same time, he always kept a gun close by, even in bed, W. D. remembered.

It was a miserable existence. "Every minute of your life you expect to get shot, run down by the police some way or another," W. D. told reporter Kent Biffle decades later. There was no real escape, especially for Clyde, who was so determined to stay out of prison, he said. "You done slipped up and done something you shouldn't have done. Then, you don't know what to do about it."

The stress made them all a little edgy. Clyde and Buck both had tempers that could flare quickly, though Buck was by far the bigger hothead; he also drank a fair bit, which amplified his anger.

The brothers fought over whether to rob banks (Buck) or stores (Clyde), who was in charge (mostly Clyde), and who would drive while the others literally sat on top of one another in a cramped car for hours on end. Sometimes, their differences escalated to fistfights.

Bonnie and Blanche, both twenty-two years old, were increasingly at odds as well. They had been close friends when their men were in prison, but more and more they were competitive and critical of each other, especially when both were defending their partners. In an interview, Blanche once compared it to "two women in the same kitchen—there can only be one queen bee."

———————◦———————

Even when the Barrow clan tried to lie low, they couldn't seem to avoid trouble.

In late April, Dillard Darby had gone home to his boarding house in Ruston, Louisiana, for lunch, carelessly leaving his keys in his new Chevrolet. The outlaws passed by soon after, and Clyde asked W. D. to steal the car. Seeing the keys, W. D. hopped in, gave a wave, and hit the gas.

Darby ran out to try to stop him. Left in the dust, he called out to another boarding house renter, Sophia Stone. They jumped into her car and tried to chase W. D. but eventually realized they couldn't catch up.

They turned around but were stopped by an angry Clyde. He, too, had lost W. D., and he blamed Darby and Stone for ruining their plans to raid a bank. Clyde smacked Darby in the back of the head with his pistol, hard enough to break the skin. Bonnie pulled Stone from the car by her hair.

Darby, who was married, and Stone, who was engaged, were ordered into the front seat. With a full car, Clyde drove around northern Louisiana searching for W. D. but couldn't find him. Finally, he headed into southern Arkansas, still looking for him, stopping only for gas. Apparently, however, their teen accomplice had taken the opportunity to make a break for home.

Buck repeatedly threatened Darby and Stone from the backseat, but Bonnie enjoyed the company, asking them questions. Stone was the parish home demonstration agent, and she taught rural women how to stretch their dollars with home-making skills like growing vegetables, canning, and making bread. Bonnie was so hungry that she asked Stone to describe the food that she had prepared that day.

As the group sped along the muddy roads, ammunition clips repeatedly fell out of the glove box, and Clyde finally asked Stone to hold them. As the afternoon passed, Bonnie said, they "got to liking" the pair.

Bonnie was tickled to learn that Darby was an undertaker. "I know we're going to get it sooner or later," she told him. "I know you would enjoy embalming us.

"Promise us you will," she added, laughing.

Years later, Sophia Stone Cook remembered, "Clyde didn't see the humor."

Finally, the hostages were let go in rural Arkansas in the

early evening. Clyde started to drive off and then stopped to give them $5 to help them get home. The pair got a lift into the nearest town and finally arrived back home that night. "Neither of us is much worse for the experience," Darby told the newspaper the next day.

For Clyde and Bonnie, however, life on the road was about to get much, much worse.

Clyde and Bonnie share a kiss, a moment likely posed for the camera, 1933.

12

WELLINGTON, TEX., JUNE 10, 1933.—

———◇———

The road was so dimly lighted;
There were no highway signs to guide;
But they made up their minds
If all roads were blind,
They wouldn't give up till they died.

—Bonnie Parker, "The Story of Bonnie and Clyde"

NOT LONG after W. D. took off, Clyde, Bonnie, Blanche, and Buck slid into the Barrow filling station in Dallas one evening.

Without leaving the car, the outlaws chatted with Henry and Cumie. Clyde was hoping to find W. D., but he hadn't yet shown back up at the Barrows' station.

Cumie had her own agenda. "I begged Buck to stay," she wrote later, apparently hoping that she could save at least one of her sons. She believed it was still possible for Buck and Blanche to put the blame for the Joplin carnage on Clyde, and Clyde said he was willing to sign a statement saying so.

But Buck, sounding like Clyde just a few weeks before, told his mother, "There isn't a chance in the world" that he could avoid the electric chair. He would stay with his brother.

Back on the road, Clyde and Buck tried again to rob some banks. On May 12, the pair attempted to surprise the cashiers at the Lucerne State Bank in Lucerne, Indiana, but the employees quickly grabbed their own guns. Thwarted, the brothers took off in a waiting car with Bonnie and Blanche.

Their escape was as treacherous as the failed holdup. On the way out of town, an older man threw a large piece of wood in front of their car, hoping to cause an accident. Clyde was able to swerve into someone's yard and then back onto the road.

In front of a church, many residents of the small community had gathered to see what was going on, and Clyde had to slow down. According to family members, both Buck and Bonnie refused Clyde's order to open fire at the crowd.

But news accounts told a very different story. The bandits "literally shot up the town," said the *Logansport Pharos-Tribune*, resembling "the wildest escapades of Chicago gangland" or "tales of the wild and woolly west."

Gunfire spewed from the car indiscriminately. A bullet grazed the arm of one twenty-two-year-old woman. Two bullets came through the walls of another woman's bedroom, and flying fragments struck her in the cheek and shoulder. One shot passed through a telephone pole and yet another burrowed into a cherry tree.

Witnesses reported seeing both a blonde woman and a brown-haired one in the car, and they were certain they were the shooters: "Those who saw the bandits leave town were alike in their stories that the women did a large part of the shooting and probably all of it during the parting fusillade." If true, it's one of the few bits of proof of Bonnie and Blanche firing guns during a crime.

Northwest of town, Clyde ran into a herd of about twenty pigs in the road. He managed to plow through them, killing two in the process.

The failed robbery and subsequent shooting got little attention outside of the area. But a May 1933 memo by the US Bureau of Investigation noted that a woman had done the shooting. "Bonnie Parker is a gun-woman, and it was she probably who shot and killed the Ft. Worth Deputy Sheriff" in January, an agent wrote, guessing at who had done what.

The next week, the two couples robbed an Okabena, Minnesota, bank of at least $1,400. Once again, a woman and a man fired dozens of rounds from the rear car windows all the way out of town, even threatening a horse-drawn school bus with more than two dozen children on board. (However, based on eyewitness identification, two brothers and one of their wives—not the Barrows—were mistakenly convicted for that robbery and sent to prison.)

Not long after the Okabena heist, Blanche took a bus into Dallas to gather up the family for a reunion of sorts, with a plan to meet Clyde, Bonnie, and Buck in a town about an hour to the east. Blanche had some spending money from the robbery, but it wasn't all in bills. Almost half of their haul was in silver dollars.

Often, when Clyde and Bonnie wanted to meet family, they would drive by the Barrow station at night and throw a Coca-Cola bottle with a note inside it detailing a meeting place. Then Cumie would call some of the other Barrow kids and Emma Parker to tell them she had red beans cooking. That code—in case someone was listening in—alerted them to a coming visit.

Ahead of this family gathering, Blanche bought herself some tall riding boots and a pair of slim-fitting pants. With silver dollars jingling in their pockets, Clyde's younger brother, L. C., and sister Marie went shopping for dresses and men's clothes for Clyde and Bonnie. There was enough money for them to buy some things for themselves, too, and Marie picked out a blue suit that fit her just right.

Their relatives were so excited to meet up with Buck, Clyde, and Bonnie that they forgot the fried chicken and red beans they usually brought for these gatherings. Bonnie loved Marie's suit and wanted one for herself; Marie graciously took Bonnie to a private spot and exchanged clothes with her.

Clyde was generous with Marie, too. She was about to turn fifteen, and her brother gave her money to buy her first bedroom furniture—a bed, a chest of draw-

Clyde with his youngest sister, Marie, November 1933.

ers, and a dresser. It had been a tough year for her. Clyde and Buck were running for their lives, and all spring, one of her teachers happily welcomed her to school each day with a mean-spirited question: "Well, have they caught your brothers yet?"

The family was entertained with stories of their time on the road. Clyde razzed Blanche about her new boots, saying they would be hard to run in—and, remembering Joplin, running was what she usually did well.

Blanche had the whole family in stitches with her description of an argument between Clyde and Bonnie that had escalated until Bonnie demanded Clyde stop the car. She threw her clothes in a paper sack and stomped off down the road, saying she was going home.

Clyde thought it was funny for a while—until she didn't return. He followed her into a cornfield, weaving up and down the rows, pleading with her. Finally, Clyde picked her up and brought her back to the car, kicking and screaming. The bag tore and her clothes were spread from one row to another. Buck had to gather her things while Clyde tried to kiss and make up.

Before the reunion was over, the family tried again to get Buck to turn himself in. Emma Parker took Bonnie for a walk to beg her to do the same. Both mothers believed a prison sentence was better than what was likely ahead.

Neither Buck nor Bonnie would budge. Buck didn't see any other options. And Bonnie simply wanted to be with Clyde. "I love him and I'm going to be with him till the end," she told her mother. "When he dies, I want to die anyway.

Clyde cleans guns while he and Bonnie are on the road, circa 1934.

LEGEND HAS IT: KEEPING UP WITH CLYDE AND BONNIE

Long before cell phones, texts, and email, Clyde and Bonnie managed to stay in fairly close touch with their families. Others also were able to find them, even as they hopscotched around the country.

How?

Clyde and Bonnie sent occasional postcards from their travels, sometimes unsigned, sometimes with made-up names. Usually, the notes assured their families that they were okay, though they occasionally included vaguely coded messages. Sometimes, the couple sent word with others. And they regularly came through Dallas to meet up with family.

It helped that West Dallas was a small community where just about everyone knew one another's business. The Barrows knew W. D.'s family and Raymond Hamilton's mom and stepdad, among others.

When the Dallas police finally tapped the Barrow family telephone for a couple of weeks, transcripts showed that Cumie and Marie Barrow chatted regularly with neighbors and friends, including Emma Parker and Billie Parker Mace. They made plans and exchanged news, such as who was in jail and why.

When friends or partners-in-crime wanted to find the outlaws, they left a message with Cumie or Henry at the station on Eagle Ford Road. Some sought out Billie or Clyde's younger siblings, L. C. and Marie, who often could be found at a local dance hall.

"Let's don't be sad," she went on. "I'm happy just being with Clyde, no matter what comes."

As the gathering broke up, the outlaws left more of their bounty with family: $112 for Mrs. Parker (about $2,000 today), $30 for Blanche's mother, and "a few hundred dollars" for the Barrows.

A relaxed visit with so much laugher was a welcome break for everyone. Maybe it should have been more serious, Blanche said later, but "we had to laugh to keep from crying."

——————◦——————

Soon after the family visit, Buck and Blanche headed to western Oklahoma to visit her father for a few days, and Clyde and Bonnie slipped into Dallas once more. This time, they found W. D., who rejoined them—maybe voluntarily, maybe not.

The Barrow brothers had arranged to meet up at a bridge near Sayre, Oklahoma, in the far-west part of the state, close to the Texas panhandle. On June 10, Clyde, Bonnie, and W. D. were late, and as usual, Clyde was driving at breakneck speed on a new road near Wellington, Texas. It was dark, and he missed the detour sign directing him to the old road. The new bridge had not yet been built.

Realizing the danger too late, Clyde slammed the brakes. But he wasn't fast enough. Suddenly, the car was airborne, hurtling toward the riverbed. "Hold your hats! It might not have a bottom," he warned.

Two men enjoying homemade ice cream on the porch of a nearby farmhouse saw the crash and came running. Clyde and

W. D. were banged up, bleeding, and shaken, but alert. Bonnie, however, was unconscious and seriously injured. Acid from the car battery had splattered on her, badly burning her leg around and below the knee.

Clyde and W. D. began to gather up as many guns as they could, and Clyde asked one of the men to carry Bonnie to the nearby house. There, two women gently put her on a bed and began to clean her up, applying salve on the burn and washing dirt and sand from her face and hair.

One of the men begged them to call a doctor, but Clyde wouldn't hear of it.

"We can't afford it," he told them, making an excuse to avoid an encounter with law enforcement.

While Bonnie was being tended to, one of the men in the house slipped out to summon the sheriff. Clyde returned to the car to retrieve more of their things, while W. D. stood guard outside with a gun.

Everyone was nervous. One of the women in the house, who was holding her four-month-old baby on her hip, moved to latch a door. Seeing her move, a quick-trigger W. D. fired through the window, sending buckshot into her hand.

Clyde heard the woman's screams and returned, noticing that one man was missing. He and W. D. waited outside for the sheriff to arrive. There wasn't anything else they could do—they didn't have a car and they couldn't run.

In town, county sheriff George Corry got the message that three people were badly injured. He and the town marshal, Paul Hardy, hurried to the house to help. "I thought they were probably a couple of drunks," Corry said. He was surprised when he and Hardy walked from the back to the front of the house and into the barrels of two guns.

Clyde and W. D. took them hostage, and Bonnie, awakened by the commotion, hobbled outside. After loading the officers into Corry's Chevrolet, Clyde shot out the tires of the farm family's car so that they couldn't follow.

Before he left, though, Clyde offered to pay the family "for all the trouble we've been to you." The family declined. "If a man can't help another man, things are in pretty bad shape," one of them said.

Bonnie started off in the front seat but was soon moved to the back, with her head in Hardy's lap. Later, she said that Hardy treated her with unusual care and kindness, calming her and trying to protect her from the bumps and jolts of the road.

In the early hours of June 11, Clyde finally made it to his meeting place with Buck, who was there waiting with Blanche. Pulling Buck aside, he told his brother about their perilous situation: He thought Bonnie was dying. And he had two policemen with him.

"Are we going to kill those men?" Buck asked.

"No," Clyde told him, impressed with how gentle they had been with Bonnie. "I have been with them so long, I'm beginning to like them."

He and Buck used Corry's handcuffs to link the two men together and then tied them to a tree with barbed wire. The lawmen were able to free themselves as the sun was coming up.

Blanche was worried that Bonnie, Clyde, and W. D. might all

die. Bonnie was writhing in pain, Clyde and W. D. were cut up and hurting, and they were all bloody. Bonnie was barefoot and Clyde, who liked to drive in his socks, was missing a shoe.

As daylight spread across the horizon, the five of them headed to Kansas, where they rented a tourist cabin for a couple days. Clyde and W. D. began to recover, but Bonnie was still in terrible pain.

They moved on to a motel in Fort Smith, Arkansas, near the Oklahoma border, where Bonnie took a turn for the worse. She grew feverish and delirious and regularly called for her mother. Her injury was gruesome. Bone was exposed in some areas, and her leg was pulled up toward her body from the damage.

The motel owners were generous, bringing Bonnie lunch, and Clyde was able to get a local doctor to provide medicine and bandage her. The doctor recommended they hire a nurse to care for her wounds if they refused to go to a hospital.

Police in Dallas heard about the crash from Wellington officials and felt certain Clyde would ditch Bonnie somewhere because her injuries would be too much trouble. But in truth, he rarely left her side. He fed her and carried her to the bathroom, and also got hold of a powerful sedative, Amytal. It made Bonnie irritable when it wore off, but it dulled the pain and allowed her to get some rest.

A week later, though, she wasn't any better. Distraught and fearful that the end was near, Clyde drove all night to Dallas. It was especially risky because he thought local law enforcement might be looking for his return.

"He rolled up to the house and told us Bonnie was about to

die," Bonnie's sister, Billie Parker Mace, remembered later.

Clyde was afraid to bring Bonnie's mother because he was certain local police were watching her. So Billie, the single mother of two small children, agreed to go instead, and they hurried back to Fort Smith right away.

Bonnie "was out of her head for days," Billie said. "She thought I was Mother." Even as Billie nursed her sister, Clyde stayed close by, except for trips into town for groceries and drug-store items.

In need of more money to pay for medicine, bandages, the nurse, and the motel, Buck and W. D. scouted places around the area to hold up. On June 23, after robbing a grocery store north of Fort Smith, Buck was hauling down the highway at a high speed, the breeze through the windows cooling the unusually hot day. Right after topping a hill, he crashed into a slower mov-ing car, knocking it into a ditch. The impact left both him and W. D. bruised and scraped. When the sting of the crash subsided, Buck and W. D. grabbed their guns.

Town marshal Henry D. Humphrey and a deputy sheriff, Red Salyers, were driving in the opposite direction looking for the grocery bandits. They had just passed the two cars on the road; hearing the loud collision, they turned around.

As the officers' maroon Ford pulled up and Humphrey stepped out, Buck and W. D. both fired, hitting him three times with enough power to knock him off the road. He would survive only three days before dying from his wounds.

Salyers got off a few shots and then hurried to a nearby farmhouse for cover. W. D. and Buck moved to steal his car. Salyers took aim from a distance and managed to shoot off the tips of two of W. D.'s fingers. Despite the injury, W. D. and Buck got away.

When Clyde heard the story, he realized the group had to get out of town—fast. They packed up their things, and he took the motel's sheets and blankets, leaving $10 on a chest to pay for them. To reduce suspicion he split up the group. First he drove Bonnie, Blanche, and Billie to the woods some miles away. Then he went back for Buck and W. D.

By the time the steamy summer sun reappeared the next morning, they were all in Oklahoma. Their recuperation time was over.

HENRY D. HUMPHREY, 1882–1933

Henry D. Humphrey, Alma, Arkansas, town marshal.

Henry Humphrey, fifty-one years old, had been elected town marshal in the spring and had started the $15-a-month job on May 1.

He, too, was a farmer who was struggling. Because the marshal was essentially a night watchman, he could keep farming and helping with repairs and odd jobs at the local high school.

Mourners overflowed at his funeral at the First Baptist Church in Alma, Arkansas.

Humphrey left behind a wife, a son, two daughters, five sisters, and a brother. Without him, his wife had to sell the farm. "It was hard on all of us," recalled his son, Vernon, who was twenty-eight when his father died.

13

PLATTE CITY, MO., JULY 19, 1933.—

———o———

SOMETIMES

Across the fields of yesterday
She sometimes comes to me
A little girl just back from play
the girl I used to be
And yet she smiles so wistfully
once she has crept within
I wonder if she hopes to see
the woman I might have been—

—poem found among Blanche Barrow's papers, dated 1933,
a revised version of an original poem by Thomas S. Jones, Jr.

JUNE 1933 was a turning point for Clyde and Bonnie.

Bonnie's terrible burns were slow to heal, and her leg never worked properly again. As they moved on from Arkansas, she still needed help with basic tasks and couldn't get in and out of the car herself.

Their crimes were getting more national attention. Clyde was listed in the "Line Up" section of fugitives wanted for murder in the May and September issues of *True Detective Mysteries.*

The US Bureau of Investigation stepped up its pursuit, especially after finding about three hundred rounds of ammunition in the wrecked car near Wellington, Texas.

The bureau's interest was further heightened on June 17, a week after the Wellington debacle, when a horrific shoot-out between unknown outlaws and lawmen at Kansas City's Union Station left three police officers and a federal agent dead, along with an escaped inmate they were escorting.

The shooting led the new Roosevelt administration to declare a "war on crime" in response to shootings, bank robberies, and kidnappings during the Depression. Until then, the Bureau of Investigation, led by J. Edgar Hoover, had primarily identified fingerprints and traced stolen cars that crossed state lines. Eager to expand his empire and win more attention and funding, Hoover began to beef up his staff and take on a greater role in pursuing criminals, a job that had previously belonged to city, county, and state lawmen. The notorious crimes of the Barrow brothers, along with Pretty Boy Floyd and, soon, John Dillinger, would help raise Hoover's profile.

Meanwhile, Clyde and Bonnie were trying to avoid any law enforcement—local, state, or otherwise. Bonnie was finally improving. Hoping to keep her sister, Billie, out of trouble, the group dropped her off at a train station in north Texas with money for the fare home and some new clothes.

The outlaws hid out again in Oklahoma for a bit. On July 7, Clyde and Buck raided another National Guard armory in Enid, Oklahoma. They "brought back so many guns that it looked like a gun factory," W. D. said later. There were dozens of pistols, some rifles and B.A.R.s, and cases of ammunition.

On July 18, the five relocated to the Red Crown tourist court near Platte City, Missouri, about twenty miles north of Kansas City. The spot, at the intersection of two highways, had a popular tavern and dance hall nearby and a grocery store and filling station across the street. Blanche rented two cabins with two garages in between for $4, paying in small change.

Almost immediately, the newcomers attracted attention. They put newspapers on their windows to block out snoopers, even though daytime temperatures reached the mid-eighties. They bought five meals at a time, sometimes spending as much as $10.

Blanche went to the Platte City drugstore to buy bandages and syringes for Bonnie. Her purchases raised the eyebrows of the pharmacist, and her riding boots and pants caught the eye of locals who hung out at the soda fountain. "We didn't see many strangers, so you can see how this particular stranger—a rather good-looking gal dressed in a slinky riding habit—attracted considerable attention," one longtime local said later.

By the next day, Sheriff Holt Coffey was pretty sure he had the Barrow gang in his county. Knowing they were dangerous, he quickly began to round up help from surrounding counties. He called the sheriff in nearby Kansas City to ask for equipment and men, but he got a chilly reception. "I'm getting pretty damn tired of every hick sheriff in the country coming in here telling me they have a bunch of desperadoes holed up and wanting help," Coffey said the sheriff told him. Only after some negotiation did the sheriff agree to loan him a bulletproof car and other support.

By that evening, Coffey had pulled together at least a dozen lawmen, a couple of submachine guns, the armored car, and a metal shield or two for protection.

Sometime after 11 P.M., the officers made their move. A deputy pulled the armored car up near one garage. Then Sheriff Coffey knocked on the door of Blanche and Buck's cabin and asked to talk with one of the men. Blanche told him she needed to get dressed first.

Clyde, hearing the conversation, looked out the window and saw the armored car and assembled officers. Sheriff Coffey was turned toward Buck's cabin, holding a steel shield.

With his B.A.R. Clyde sent a stream of bullets into the armored car, which turned out to be less-than-bulletproof. The military weapon pierced the car's armor, and the driver was shot in both legs. Another shot hit the horn, which began to blare repeatedly. A deputy in the car, seeing blood, put the car in reverse and helped his partner back it up as the other policemen unleashed a torrent of ammunition at the two cabins and the garages. The officers' submachine guns jammed, however, rendering them useless.

Locals who had gathered to witness the fireworks suddenly found themselves awfully close to the shooting. Clarence Coffey, the sheriff's nineteen-year-old son, started out watching from the front of the tavern with a waitress. When a shot knocked his father off-balance, he wanted to go help. But before he could move, he was hit in the upper arm and another bullet traveled across his scalp. Other rounds grazed him, and he lost consciousness.

When he came to, he found the waitress had pulled him inside the tavern. "I looked at her and thought she was bleeding to death, but it was my blood spraying on her," he said later.

Bonnie and W. D. managed to grab a few things and get into the garage where the car was parked. Clyde opened the garage door for Blanche and Buck. But before they could get there, a bullet tore into Buck's head on the left side, exiting his forehead. He stumbled, and Blanche and Clyde helped lift him into the car.

Despite the gunfire, Clyde was able to pull out of the garage and slip by a truck intended to block their exit.

On the way out, more bullets ripped into their car and a shot shattered the plate-glass rear window, sending shards flying. Some glass pierced Blanche's eyes, dimming her vision; something else hit the side of her head. Bonnie's burn wound had reopened. The insides of the cabins were demolished and the outsides were pockmarked, but Clyde and W. D. were relatively unscathed.

Souvenir hunters look for bullet holes at the Red Crown tourist court the day after the July 19, 1933, shoot-out.

The escape "was quite a spectacular thing. No one could believe that it could happen," Clarence Coffey said later.

No officers tried to chase them. Their guns were no match for the military weapons stolen from the National Guard armory. As a Bureau of Investigation agent had written in a memo just a few days before: "unless peace officers are equipped with similar weapons and experienced in the use of them, it is practically suicide for anyone to attempt to combat or capture criminals who use Browning Automatic Rifles."

As they sped away, Blanche cradled Buck in her lap. He was bleeding, she was bleeding, and Bonnie was hurting. Clyde struggled to exit the Platte City area. He had to stop several times to repair tires and care for their various injuries. He tried to wash out Blanche's eyes and clean Buck's head wound, which was located in the front part of the brain that affects emotion and reasoning, but was not fatal. By morning, they were still near Kansas City, fewer than ten miles from the shoot-out.

On Thursday, July 20, Clyde managed to drive the ailing group into Iowa. At a stop in the southern part of the state, a farmer saw them burning bloody clothes and bandages. Finally, they found refuge in a wooded area by an abandoned park near Dexter, Iowa, that had featured a ball field, dance hall, and swimming pool before the Depression.

Back in Dallas, the Barrows' latest escape was big news. "Luck must be with them," Raymond Hamilton told a reporter in an interview at the Dallas County jail. "But it won't be long before they lose their rabbit's foot."

Hamilton was being held in solitary confinement before he could be transferred to prison. Even though he was facing a sentence of 263 years for robberies and the murder of John Bucher in Hillsboro, he told the reporter he was better off than Clyde and Buck. "Either of them is liable to be killed any day," he added.

At the Barrow gas station, Cumie was in tears. "They're living on borrowed time," the fifty-eight-year-old mother told a deputy sheriff and a Dallas reporter who stopped by. "I know that as well as you do."

Standing with Buck's oldest child, ten-year-old Marvin, she told the men that the boy hadn't seen his daddy in years. She had carefully followed the news accounts of the shootings in Joplin, Alma, and near Platte City, and she knew that officers would rather kill them than arrest them.

————◆————

In the ninety-degree heat, Clyde set up camp for his injured family on a hill in a wooded area in, ironically, Dallas County, Iowa, about thirty miles due west of Des Moines. Despite his serious head injury, Buck was able to talk and eat. Blanche was more rattled. A piece of glass was still stuck in one eye and she was panicking about Buck's condition. She didn't leave his side.

At some point, Clyde and W. D. stole another car, so they wouldn't have to explain the multiple bullet holes in their first vehicle. Every day Clyde drove into Dexter for the basics. On Friday, July 21, he stopped at John Love's shop to buy a couple of new shirts and some new shoes. Initially, the young man was friendly and relaxed, Love remembered. But after Love fetched the shirts and some black shoes, "I noticed he was just staring a hole right through me."

Clyde paid quickly and scooted out. He had seen Love's deputy badge pinned inside a pocket.

The outlaw stopped at a restaurant and market to order five dinners, taking dishes and silverware with him, and then went to a nearby pharmacy for alcohol, gauze, and burn ointment. He came back on Saturday and Sunday for more meals and more supplies, returning the china and utensils each time. By the end of the weekend, the shopkeepers were asking questions about the polite, pleasant-looking stranger.

Out by the campsite, farmers, too, had begun to notice the

visitors. One had seen partially burned bloody clothing and used bandages. The locals called John Love. He came out to take a look and notified the county sheriff.

"You missin' any damned outlaws?" he asked.

"Yes, the whole Barrow gang" came the reply.

"Then you better get your heavy artillery and come out here," Love told him.

The sheriff began to assemble lawmen, including police officers from Des Moines and other towns, and sheriffs and vigilantes from several counties. They gathered Sunday night, along with dozens of thrill seekers, who wanted a front seat at the confrontation. More than a few were drinking and some even showed up with dates.

When the sun came up on July 24, the posse started to make its move. Love could see W. D. cooking hot dogs over a fire in the distance. Bonnie looked up and saw men approaching, perhaps one hundred yards away. Hoping to force the posse to back off, Clyde fired a round from his B.A.R. into the trees, dropping limbs and brush onto the lawmen. One shot rippled along a deputy's forehead. Some officers hit the dirt and fired back; others retreated.

W. D. stood and caught buckshot in the chest.

Racing to beat the bullets, Clyde ordered everyone into the car. W. D. was hit again, but managed to get in. Bonnie helped Blanche and Buck, while Clyde kept shooting. Sliding behind the wheel, he managed to drive a bit before hitting a dead end.

Clyde was shot in the shoulder as he threw the car into reverse. Unable to control the wheel, he backed over a stump. The car hung, unmovable.

The five started to head toward their other car, but the

lawmen had already demolished it with a huge round of artil-lery. So they turned into the woods, buckshot chasing them. Bonnie took two pellets in her stomach, W. D. was struck again, and Buck was hit in the back.

Though bleeding profusely, W. D. picked up Bonnie and car-ried her. Buck urged Clyde to leave him and take Blanche.

Blanche wouldn't hear of it, nor would Clyde.

Clyde grabbed both Blanche and Buck and pulled them through the brush until they reached a fence.

As they pushed up a hill, Buck could go no farther, and he and Blanche fell behind. Clyde, Bonnie, and W. D. continued on until they were near a river. Spotting a bridge, Clyde urged them to hide in the brush while he tried to run for a car. W. D. and Bonnie burrowed down among briars and thorns. Blanche helped Buck hide behind a huge fallen tree near the old ball field.

When Clyde got close to the bridge, he saw it, too, was guarded with lawmen. He tried to shoot, but he couldn't control his heavy military weapon with his injured shoulder, and missed wildly. A sharpshooting deputy returned fire, knocking the B.A.R. from his hands and clipping his cheek. Clyde emptied the last rounds from his pistol and disappeared back into the brush.

When the yelling and the shooting suddenly stopped, Bonnie froze at the deadly silence.

"I knew they'd got Clyde," she told her family. "My heart turned to ice. Nothing else mattered—my wounds—my leg—death—nothing." She couldn't hold back the tears.

Several minutes later—it felt like forever—she heard a hiss, and Clyde reappeared, crawling and blood-soaked from several wounds. They hugged and kissed and then confronted their situation. There were no other options, he told them. They would have to try to cross the nearby river.

With Bonnie on W. D.'s back, they eased down a steep, heavily wooded hill and plunged into the water. On the other side, they climbed up another hill and Clyde clawed through a cornfield toward a barn, holding his wet and empty gun.

A farmer and his nineteen-year-old son were beginning their day when the muddy, bloodstained young man pointed his .45 at them. Clyde told them he didn't want to hurt anyone—he just needed their car. Then he whistled for W. D. and Bonnie.

Bonnie was gently placed in the backseat of their four-year-old Plymouth. W. D. climbed in next to her, and Clyde slid behind the wheel. Around 6 A.M. they were off, in search of a new place to hide.

Back at the park, the lawmen were moving carefully and deliberately, trying not to trigger the heavy firepower of the outlaws they were chasing.

Finally, two hours after Clyde, Bonnie, and W. D. had departed, searchers spotted a huge felled tree that looked like a good hiding place.

As two men moved toward the spot, Buck was ready, aiming his automatic pistol. A local dentist and National Guardsman shot first, catching Buck in the shoulder.

Blanche screamed.

Other lawmen rushed to help. Two men carried the injured Buck the equivalent of a few blocks to an open space. Another man led Blanche, who was beside herself with grief and fear. When they set Buck down, she leaned over him.

"Daddy, Daddy, are you all right?"

"Sure, baby, I'm all right," Buck said quietly.

But he wasn't. The bandage was missing from his head and brain tissue was pushing out of his wound. He was shot in the shoulder and the back.

Inside the two stolen cars, officers found a Bible and a veritable armory: more than thirty automatic pistols, as well as a pile of ammunition. Among clothes and bandages that the group had tried to burn, they also found a blood-soaked copy of *Country Gentleman* magazine, stolen from a mailbox and used as a seat cushion.

As soon as Buck and Blanche were taken away, souvenir hunters descended on their campsite, plucking bullets out of trees and searching for anything they could take. The slippery young outlaws apparently were as fascinating as they were violent and dangerous.

Somehow, some way, Clyde and Bonnie had managed to escape three intense efforts to blast them into oblivion. Now they were bleeding and wounded and their future looked terribly grim.

Police hold a hysterical Blanche (at left), while others crouch around a badly wounded Buck, who is curled up on the ground, after the shoot-out near Dexter, Iowa, July 24, 1933.

14

DES MOINES, IOWA, JULY 1933.—

———————o———————

The road gets dimmer and dimmer;

Sometimes you can hardly see;

But, it's fight, man to man,

And do all you can,

For they know they can never be free.

—Bonnie Parker, "The Story of Bonnie and Clyde"

CONSIDERING HIS ghastly injuries, Buck was surprisingly alert and talkative. Blanche was less so.

Officers first took them to a doctor, where Buck was examined and glass was removed from Blanche's eye. Buck was taken to a local hospital, while Blanche was transported to jail.

There she was fingerprinted, weighed (a mere eighty-one pounds), and measured (five feet one inch in her riding boots).

"Was your husband with you?" asked a Des Moines police officer.

"Yes," she answered.

"Who else was with you?"

"Jack Sherman," she replied, using a fake name for W. D. Police had yet to figure out who he was, despite the Joplin photographs,

Blanche's eye was treated and bandaged after the July 24 shoot-out before she was taken back to Missouri to face charges.

and her answers wouldn't help.

Posse members had reported that a woman fired at them that morning. "Mrs. Barrow, some of the boys say you contributed to all the hell that was out there. Did you do any shooting?" the officer asked.

"No, sir," she told him, which was probably true, given her eye injury. "I didn't do anything. There was plenty of hell but I didn't contribute to it."

The officer asked her reaction to the events that morning.

"I figured it was the end," she replied.

Back in Dallas, Sheriff Schmid visited the Barrow filling station to tell Cumie and Henry that their older son was in the hospital with life-threatening wounds.

Cumie broke into sobs. "I've got to see my boy!" she cried, according to a Dallas newspaper. "I just know that if I don't see Buck before he dies, I'll never get to see either of them alive again."

Both parents asked about Clyde.

"Of course, I know you think they are bad boys," Henry said to Schmid. "But they are our boys."

Henry and Cumie also asked how Blanche and Bonnie were, as well as the other man with Buck and Clyde. But like Blanche, they were evasive, refusing to offer any details. "I just can't figure out who he is," Henry said.

Schmid gave Cumie a written note that introduced her as Buck's mother. Later, Bonnie's sister, Billie Parker Mace, said that a deputy sheriff provided some of the funds that allowed her, Cumie, Emma Parker, and L. C. Barrow to make the long drive to Iowa.

While the family hurried to Buck's side, a parade of lawmen questioned Buck at the hospital. Two officers from Alma, Arkansas, including Red Salyers, came to his bedside to ask about the recent murder of Henry Humphrey. Buck readily admitted shooting the town marshal and recognized Salyers. "You were lucky you got out of my way," he said.

In an interview with a Bureau of Investigation agent and an Iowa sheriff, he denied raiding a National Guard armory, but he confessed to three filling station robberies. He seemed to be in good spirits, the federal agent reported.

"Even though realizing that he probably did not have long to live, he, on several occasions, laughed heartily about some of his escapades," the agent wrote. Doctors did not expect Buck to survive, which was obvious to the lawmen. His head wound had become infected, the agent noted, and it "gave off such an offensive odor that it was with the utmost difficulty that one could remain within several feet of him."

Someone asked why Buck was so quick to take the life of another person.

"Well," he answered, "I had to see that I did not get hurt."

By the time Cumie arrived on Wednesday, his fever was 105 degrees.

"Oh darling! My baby! Speak to me!" she begged.

"I knew you'd come, Mother. Kiss me," Buck rasped back.

She kept a vigil by his bedside as he fell into a coma the next day. On Saturday, July 29, ten days after he was shot in the head, Marvin Ivan "Buck" Barrow died. He was thirty years old. In four months' time, he had been involved in three murders, four shoot-outs, and the kidnapping of two people. He left behind a trail of too many robberies and burglaries to count, loving parents and siblings, two children from two marriages, and Blanche, who was being held in a Missouri jail on a bond of $15,000 (more than $275,000 today). She would plead guilty to assault with intent to kill during the Platte City, Missouri, shoot-out in September, and receive a ten-year sentence in a Missouri prison. While there, doctors operated at least twice to save the sight in her left eye but weren't successful.

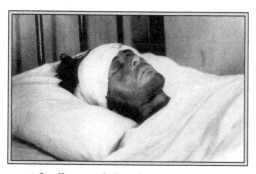

A fatally wounded Buck Barrow in a Des Moines hospital, July 1933.

Buck was buried in West Dallas on July 31, following a quiet funeral. The Barrows held off buying a headstone; they figured they would soon be burying another son. When Cumie was in Iowa, she was asked if she would beg Clyde to turn himself in.

"No," she replied. "I feel that either way, Clyde has only a few days to live.

"If he remains at large, officers will shoot him in their attempts to capture him. If he surrenders, he will face execution.

"So," she said, "I'm going to let him live his last few days the way he wants to, without any instructions or pleas from me."

LEGEND HAS IT: BUCK'S FUNERAL

Clyde, Bonnie, and W. D. weren't in much shape to travel after the Dexter, Iowa, shoot-out. But according to legend, Clyde snuck into Buck's funeral dressed as an old woman with gray hair and wearing a bonnet.

The funeral was fairly small and police officers said they were watching closely for anything suspicious. Officers didn't believe Clyde was there. But the rumor was repeated in the Dallas newspapers and endured for years.

Where were Clyde, Bonnie, and W. D.?

Just about everyone in Iowa was asking, and many claimed to have seen them right after the shoot-out. But airplane surveillance, searches of abandoned farmhouses, and extensive monitoring of the roads didn't kick up anything but rumors.

Still in the Dallas jail, Raymond Hamilton predicted that Clyde and Bonnie would be tough to catch. One reason, he told reporters, is that the couple was determined to avoid capture—so much so that they had an agreement to kill each other if they thought their freedom was at stake.

"Bonnie and Clyde are in love," Raymond said. "She is jealous of him and he is jealous of her. Clyde doesn't 'gal around' any at all. Bonnie is the only girl he ever thinks about.

"They're saying they'll catch them before the end of the week," he added. "I say they're dead wrong."

Not surprisingly, Clyde was back behind the wheel. Shortly after their escape, he, Bonnie, and W. D. switched cars at a filling station, stealing a Chevrolet, which was later abandoned in Nebraska. As time passed without new crimes, some began to think they had died from their injuries. In truth, they found quiet places to camp and nursed their many wounds, which were painful but not life threatening.

In August, they replenished their arsenal by removing weapons from an Illinois National Guard armory they had robbed once before.

Sometime after that, they traveled to Mississippi, where W. D. decided he was done as an outlaw. Over eight months, he had seen a lifetime's worth of violence and crime, including five murders. "I'd had enough blood and hell," he said later. When he saw a chance, he took off alone for Texas and found work picking cotton.

For a while, W. D. later said, crime had seemed exciting and fun, but in truth, "It was torment."

Whether Clyde expected W. D.'s departure isn't clear, but this time he didn't go looking for his young accomplice. Clyde and Bonnie would stay on their deadly course without him.

Years later, those who survived would reflect on why Clyde was so quick to shoot. Clyde "never wanted to kill. He'd kidnap the police instead of killing them, if he could. But he killed without hesitation when he had to," W. D. said. "Clyde just wanted to stay alive and free, and Bonnie just wanted to be with Clyde."

Blanche saw another reason: "Fear. They weren't naturally mean. But they were afraid," she said. In fact, she added, "both Bonnie and Clyde were likeable. It was a terrible kind of life they lived. Bonnie wouldn't have done it if she hadn't loved Clyde so."

Without W. D. to help, Bonnie and Clyde survived mostly on the take from small robberies, as well as the pillows, blankets, food, and clothing that their families could provide. Bonnie was still twenty-two and Clyde was a year or two older, but both were thinner and much older looking than they had been only three months before, and there were no longer any silver dollars in their pockets.

Their situation "made living a humble life in West Dallas look good by comparison," Marie Barrow said later.

Worrying that they might not have too many opportunities left, Clyde and Bonnie found ways to spend more time with their families, despite being two of the most-wanted people in Texas after more than a year of murder and malice.

To go unrecognized near their home turf, the pair sometimes dyed their hair. Bonnie was naturally blonde or strawberry blonde, but on occasion she was red-haired, and at least once, so was Clyde. Sometimes he wore a wig, and, according to family lore, Bonnie put lipstick and makeup on him to disguise him as a woman a few times.

Despite their violent summer and the knowledge that the pair came through town regularly, the understaffed Dallas County police and sheriff's deputies did not stake out the Barrow or Parker homes, nor did they seem intent on catching Bonnie and Clyde. Perhaps the officers were just too poorly trained to know what to do—or distracted with other local crimes. There is no proof that any officers took bribes to leave them alone, but police payoffs were fairly common during Prohibition and the Depression. There was another, less-discussed reason that

Bonnie and Clyde remained free: no lawman in his right mind would try to take on a shooter with Clyde's reputation and weaponry by himself, or start a shoot-out with innocent people around. So even if Clyde were spotted in Dallas, an officer would want to call for assistance before confronting him; by the time help arrived, Clyde would be long gone.

LEGEND HAS IT: BILLIE'S BABIES

Along with Bonnie's dreadful injury and Buck's death, there were two more terrible tragedies for the families in 1933.

Billie Parker Mace's two-year-old daughter, Jackie, became ill suddenly in mid-October and died. A few days later, Billie's four-year-old son, Buddy, died as well.

The family believed the cause of death was a stomach disorder. But given the era, it could also have been a disease like typhoid or a vicious flu. Everyone was heartbroken, including Bonnie, who adored children and doted on her niece and nephew.

Still, Smoot Schmid had not forgotten about Clyde Barrow— or about the fact that he faced reelection in 1934. "It would be completely accurate to say that Sheriff Schmid wanted nothing so much in the world as to capture Clyde Barrow and Bonnie Parker and to walk them down Main Street of Dallas to show the world what he'd done," Deputy Sheriff Ted Hinton said later. Hinton said he and Deputy Bob Alcorn, who had been pursuing the pair for months, tried to convince Schmid that such an outcome was impossible. But the sheriff wouldn't listen.

The sheriff's office got a break in mid-November, when a tip finally led them to W. D. Jones, who was in the Houston area. Under questioning, W. D. poured out details about his time with Clyde and Bonnie to an assistant district attorney—albeit with some plot twists.

W. D. claimed that whenever there had been a shooting, he was either unconscious or absent. He said Clyde and Bonnie had forced him to join them and handcuffed him to trees at times so that he wouldn't run away. If a second person had fired a weapon, he told officers it was Bonnie, not him. (Years later, however, he told an interviewer that in big battles, "she never fired a gun. But I'll say she was a hell of a loader.")

W. D. mapped out his eight months of crime with the Barrow gang stop by stop, state by state. He said Clyde had killed Doyle Johnson in Temple, Texas, for Johnson's car; that was a meaningful disclosure, since another Dallas man had been accused of the crime. He detailed the gun battles in Joplin, Alma, Platte City, and Dexter, though without ever admitting to any shooting, and claiming he participated against his will.

Deputy Sheriff Hinton said later that he didn't believe W. D.'s claims, but his story was a savvy one. By refusing to admit to any real crimes, and also insisting that he was only seventeen (though he may have been older), W. D. wouldn't face the harsh penalties an adult would.

Officials also made note of the painful souvenirs from his travels: bullet wound scars on his side and his chest; a burn scar on his thigh from the Wellington car crash; scars on his face,

LEGEND HAS IT: **WAS W. D. REALLY HANDCUFFED TO CLYDE?**

In his statement to police, W. D. Jones claimed Clyde sometimes handcuffed the two of them together to keep him from escaping.

Years later, in an interview with *Dallas Morning News* reporter Kent Biffle, W. D. told a different story. Clyde never put him in a situation where he couldn't run if someone opened fire on them, he said.

But when W. D. was on lookout duty and Clyde wanted to sleep, Clyde sometimes tied himself to W. D. with string. That way, if W. D. moved suddenly, he would wake Clyde up.

"He used different methods of being alert," he said.

right hand, and left leg; and buckshot still in his little finger, chest, and lower lip.

Schmid insisted on keeping W. D.'s arrest a secret from the press. His deputy Alcorn was hearing from an informant about Clyde and Bonnie's family meetings, and Schmid believed he might be able to capture them. In the meantime, he didn't want Clyde to know they had W. D.

In early November, US Bureau of Investigation Agent Edward J. Dowd offered to coordinate with the Dallas sheriff to help him catch Clyde. But Schmid told the agent that, for the time being, he "preferred to work alone."

Dowd was not impressed with Schmid's decision; in a report, he mockingly called the sheriff "Smooth Smith."

On November 21, Clyde and Bonnie celebrated Cumie's fifty-ninth birthday with other family members on a deserted road west of Dallas near an unincorporated community called Sowers. Clyde and Bonnie were planning to leave town for a while, so they asked to meet again the next night in the same spot, something they almost never did.

The sheriff's informant knew the location and approximate time. Schmid would have his big chance to be a hero.

Ahead of the meeting, Schmid; Alcorn; Hinton; and another deputy, Ed Caster, parked their car half a mile from the families' meeting spot. Then they crouched in a ditch about seventy-five yards off the road, readying their warlike arsenal,

The Parker and Barrow families gather to celebrate Cumie's birthday, November 21, 1933. In the front, left to right: Marie Barrow, Emma Parker, and Bonnie. In back, left to right: Billie Parker Mace, Clyde, Cumie Barrow, and Marie's boyfriend, Joe Bill Francis.

which included two Thompson submachine guns, a repeating rifle, and a B.A.R.

In the early evening, with Marie Barrow's boyfriend, Joe Bill Francis, at the wheel, a car carrying Barrow and Parker family members pulled up to the spot. Not long after, another car came barreling down the gravel road. Joe Bill turned on his car's headlights.

As the second car pulled even with the first, the officers opened fire, sending a storm of bullets into the outlaws' car. The Ford's windows shattered. Clyde fired back and accelerated. In a matter of seconds, he and Bonnie were gone.

Most of the family had hit the floorboards of Joe Bill's car when the shooting started; Cumie prayed out loud. As soon as the shooting ended, Joe Bill sped away, too.

Clyde headed toward Fort Worth, pushing forward despite at least one flat tire. Some distance from the ambush, he saw another car coming down the road. He cut it off and ordered the driver and passenger out. The men refused, but Clyde was in no mood for negotiation. He shot out their rear window, convincing them to give him the car.

Clyde and Bonnie grabbed as many guns as they could and drove off. Inside their bullet-riddled car were casings from ten rounds, an assortment of clothing, makeup and medicine, a sack of pennies, and eleven license plates. Blood was on the seats, indicating at least one of them was injured. There was also a December issue of *Master Detective.* (Though there was no story about the Barrow gang in that magazine, Clyde was featured in the December *Real Detective* article, "New Bad Men of the Old Wild West," as an example of a bad man who "lived up to the daring precedent" of Jesse James and Billy the Kid.)

Because Schmid and his officers didn't have a car nearby—and had not planned for the criminals to escape—there was nothing they could do when the cars sped off. Luckily, none of them were hurt, but a woman living a half-mile away was cut in the neck when a shot from one of their military weapons broke her window.

Rather than celebrating his heroism, Schmid had to explain to the press and the public why he hadn't been better prepared. But he was able to redirect reporters' pointed criticism about his sloppy work by finally disclosing W. D. Jones's arrest and confession.

Sheriff Smoot Schmid and deputies (from left to right) Ed Caster, Ted Hinton, and Bob Alcorn show off license plates, magazines, maps, and other items found in Clyde and Bonnie's bullet-pocked car after their failed ambush attempt, November 22, 1933.

"Boys," said Schmid, "it will take you until midnight to finish this story, it's so big." Schmid's ploy mostly worked.

Despite reports that Clyde and Bonnie were gravely wounded, they weren't seriously hurt. A bullet had injured both of them in the knee and leg. Bonnie would have difficulty standing unassisted again.

Retreating to one of their Oklahoma haunts, they were able to get treatment from a doctor and a nurse. Within a week, Clyde's wounds had improved enough for them to drive back to Dallas.

Clearly someone had snitched on the couple and divulged their plans, and it almost certainly was a family member or someone very close to one. Later, some family members would speculate that Joe Bill, the driver of the other car, was the informant, but his role was never confirmed. If the Barrows and Parkers believed it was Joe Bill, they didn't seem to blame him; he married Marie Barrow a few months later.

Clyde's fiery temper was boiling again, but this time it was focused on the sheriff for putting his and Bonnie's mothers and siblings in danger. He was also angry at law enforcement in general and the whole system that was determined to kill him. So when Jimmy Mullins came calling several weeks later, Clyde was ready for the most outrageous crime of his extraordinarily violent career.

15

EASTHAM FARM, TEXAS PRISON SYSTEM, JANUARY 16, 1934.—

A newsboy once said to his buddy:
"I wish old Clyde would get jumped;
In these awful hard times
We'd make a few dimes
If five or six cops would get bumped."

—Bonnie Parker, "The Story of Bonnie and Clyde"

JIMMY MULLINS was a former drug addict who had spent much of his adult life in prison. Convicted of narcotics crimes and burglary, he served time in Illinois and Kansas prisons before landing at Texas's Eastham Farm.

At Eastham, he got to know Raymond Hamilton, who had arrived in August afloat with confidence and swagger. Raymond liked to brag that his pal Clyde Barrow would get him out, since he was serving time, in part, for a murder that Clyde knew Raymond didn't commit. Raymond's cockiness had once prompted Dallas County sheriff Schmid to warn prison officials that he was a flight risk.

The prison folks laughed at Schmid. "Hamilton is as gentle

as a male manicurist," Schmid said the prison officials told him. "He's just like any other prisoner."

But Raymond disagreed. The twenty-year-old offered Jimmy Mullins a deal: if Mullins would help get a prison break rolling, Raymond would pay him $2,000 when he got out. It was too tempting for an old jail-bird like Mullins to resist.

When Mullins was paroled on January 10, 1934, he made his way to Dallas and found

Newspaper cartoonist Jack Patton questioned how easily Clyde had been paroled from prison, January 18, 1934.

Floyd Hamilton, Raymond's older brother. He detailed a plan to bust Raymond out—one that Clyde and Ralph Fults had mapped out a couple of years before.

Floyd, uncertain about such an audacious scheme, suggested they talk to Clyde and Bonnie. The four met in a rural area west of Dallas and discussed the plan, which called for two .45 caliber automatic pistols to be hidden in the brush near where Raymond had been working.

Clyde didn't trust Mullins. But he agreed to help if Mullins and Floyd would hide the weapons on prison property.

On January 13, Clyde, Bonnie, Mullins, and Floyd drove to Eastham Farm. The weather was mild for January, in the sixties. That night, Floyd and Mullins crept to the farm and tucked an inner tube containing two pistols and ammunition under a bridge near the woodpile where the inmates had been chopping.

They returned to Clyde and Bonnie without any trouble, and the four headed back north. That Sunday morning, Floyd picked up his wife in Dallas and the couple went to Eastham to visit Raymond and alert him that the plan had been put in place.

Meanwhile, Clyde, Bonnie, and Mullins studied the roads out of the area. At night, the men slept and Bonnie kept a lookout. During the day, she got her shut-eye snuggled into the car's rounded hatchback-like trunk, known as a turtleback.

In the early morning of January 16, the weather was damp and cooler and a thick fog huddled over the fields. As usual, the inmates ran to the area where they had been chopping and stacking wood and cutting brush. Raymond Hamilton had quietly switched from his usual squad No. 2 to his friend Joe Palmer's squad No. 1, so they could team up to carry out the plan. Following procedure, the squad guard Olin Bozeman wouldn't force him back to his proper group until they got to the work site.

Once there, Bozeman called over Major Crowson, the "long arm man," whose job was to hang back near the woods with a rifle and make sure no one tried to escape. Sitting on their horses side by side, Bozeman asked Crowson to tell another guard to come get Raymond, who was out of place.

"Boy, you had better look out. That means something," Crowson told him.

Neither had a chance to move before they saw Joe Palmer just a few feet away, aiming a pistol at them. Crowson was shot first, taking a hit in the stomach that exited through his back.

Bozeman reached for his gun, and Palmer managed to shoot

it away. Bozeman's horse wheeled around, and the next shot caught the guard in the hip.

Raymond Hamilton tried to fire, but the clip fell off his gun after the first shot.

With both guards hit, Palmer, Raymond Hamilton, and two other inmates made their way into a ditch, following it until they got to the road where their pals were waiting. Worried that they might make a wrong turn in the fog, Bonnie had repeatedly hit the horn once the sound of shooting had stopped. Using automatic rifles, Clyde and Mullins had opened fire into the trees, hoping to provide cover for the escapees and discourage anyone from following them.

Once the four men emerged from the fog, they all crammed into the car, with some of the escapees hanging their feet from the turtleback.

A fifth inmate, taking advantage of the confusion, ran into the woods seeking his own freedom. He was caught within a day.

Back in the field, Crowson and Bozeman were badly injured but still on their horses. They made their way to the barracks, where they were taken to the hospital.

Before anyone could sound an alert, Clyde was on his way north, traveling on dirt roads and cutting across fields to avoid any roadblocks. Soon, reports began to spread via radio and telegraph. Near Hillsboro, about a hundred and fifty miles away, Clyde stopped for gas. An excited attendant asked him if he heard the big news.

No, he said. They hadn't.

Well, he said, Clyde and Bonnie had marched right into the Eastham dining hall and broken Raymond Hamilton out. The attendant was so chatty that Clyde finally had to ask him when they were going to get gasoline.

An early edition of the afternoon *Dallas Dispatch* told a similar embellished story: Clyde had driven up to the Eastham barracks alone, shooting three guards and rescuing Raymond Hamilton while he was at breakfast.

LEGEND HAS IT: DEAD OR ALIVE

After the prison break, the Texas legislature created a $1,000 reward (almost $20,000 today) for Clyde Barrow's capture. But lawmakers got knotted up in a long debate over whether the reward should be paid for him "dead or alive."

One legislator worried that offering such a reward would encourage mobs to attack someone on the street. Another noted, "There is no law in the Bible which authorizes us to kill a man even though he be a criminal."

Said State Representative Harry Graves, "We are attempting to do the very thing we are condemning Barrow for doing." He added, "We should not offer $1,000 to make a man a cold-blooded murderer."

The words "dead or alive" were removed.

By morning, the prison break was national news, and it was an increasingly juicy and dramatic story, raising the profile of the outlaw couple. The *New York Times* called it a "spectacular delivery" that was "perfectly executed." The escape, it reported, was aided by the "two-gun, cigar-smoking woman" Bonnie

Parker, now twenty-three years old, who pounded on the horn.

The paper added a new, unsubstantiated tidbit to the story: Clyde and Raymond were back together even though they previously had split up after a fight over Bonnie's affections.

The newly formed gang almost immediately began to rob banks, in part to raise the money owed to Mullins. Bonnie divided the money and, according to one participant, was unusually fair because she and Clyde "value friendship more than money."

Still, living in a car and traveling from place to place each day was complicated with four men and a woman. (Possibly two women—Billie may have been with them for a while as well.) Within a week, they were all fighting, and a couple of the escapees went off on their own. (One would be captured quickly and give details to investigators.)

On January 26, Clyde, Bonnie, and the remaining men headed back to the Dallas area with full pockets. That night, Mullins said later, Raymond paid him $685 of the amount owed to him for helping with the jailbreak. He also gave $500 to his brother, Floyd, who had brought new clothes for the men and Bonnie.

In mid-February, someone else joined the group: Raymond's new girlfriend, Mary O'Dare, the wife of a former partner of his who was now in prison.

Clyde and Bonnie didn't like O'Dare or trust her. They worried that she might turn them in, perhaps to get the reward money offered in several states, which totaled hundreds of dollars. Bonnie refused to let O'Dare out of her sight.

O'Dare didn't much like them, either. She wanted to eat in nice restaurants and stay in nice hotels, while her hosts wanted to stay out of view. The tension between the couples grew.

Once, after Clyde and Bonnie had a big fight, O'Dare suggested that Bonnie should drug Clyde, take his money, and leave. Bonnie didn't appreciate the advice.

On February 27, the men robbed a bank in Lancaster, Texas, south of Dallas, netting more than $4,000. Raymond wanted his girlfriend to get a cut of the money. Clyde refused. As they drove that day, Clyde watched in the rearview mirror while Raymond tried to pocket additional cash.

Clyde pulled over and frisked Raymond. He found hundreds of dollars of extra cash in his pockets.

After weeks of squabbling, the two couples parted ways in early March. But the feud didn't end. Several weeks later, after he had been captured and jailed yet again, Raymond turned the tables in an interview with a Dallas newspaper. He insisted that Bonnie, not Mary, had demanded a cut of the money.

Clyde and Bonnie had never formally responded to any mention of them in the newspapers, even when W. D. blamed them for all the shootings. But Raymond had gotten under their skin. Clyde sent

Clyde dictated this scathing letter for Raymond Hamilton to Bonnie, April 1934. The letter was sent in care of the Dallas County Jail.

him a scathing letter, written in Bonnie's neat script and intercepted in the Dallas jail in late April. "I have always taken care of Bonnie and never asked any thief to help me," Clyde said.

After he found the extra cash on Raymond, Clyde wrote, "I should have killed you then."

———————◇———————

Prison guard Major Joseph Crowson—Major was his first name, not a title—was dying from his gunshot wound. The bullet had wreaked havoc in his abdomen and then he developed pneumonia. A week after the mid-January raid, he told Texas prison director Lee Simmons that Joe Palmer had shot him and "didn't give me a dog's chance."

"Colonel Simmons," he added, "I hope you catch him and put him in the electric chair."

On January 27, Crowson died. He was thirty-three years old.

Outraged by the Eastham breakout and Crowson's death, Simmons was determined to seek justice. He wanted Joe Palmer and Raymond Hamilton to pay for the murder, and he wanted to end Clyde Barrow's seemingly endless crime spree. In early February, he turned to Frank Hamer (pronounced HAY-mer), asking him to take on the job of tracking down Clyde and Bonnie.

Hamer, who was just shy of his fiftieth birthday, had something of a mythic reputation as a gunslinger. For years, he had been a noted Texas Ranger, part of a small outfit charged primarily with defending and monitoring the Texas border with Mexico. He had been called on to control riots and investigate crimes and had participated in more than fifty Ranger gunfights with alleged criminals, smugglers, and Mexicans that resulted in the deaths of at least twenty men.

When Texas Governor Miriam "Ma" Ferguson had taken office in 1932, Hamer left the Rangers because he didn't want to work for a woman governor. He was between jobs when Simmons called.

Simmons promised Hamer that he would provide whatever support he needed and assured him that Governor Ferguson had signed off on his appointment. Simmons explained that Hamer might have to let another criminal go free in order to nail Clyde. And he had a piece of unsolicited advice:

Frank Hamer, who was hired to find the violent couple after the Eastham prison break, circa 1930.

"The thing for you to do," he told Hamer, "is put them on the spot, know you are right—and then shoot everybody in sight."

Hamer started his new job on February 10, and immediately began to try to re-create Clyde and Bonnie's movements. While Clyde and Raymond were bickering, Hamer was visiting Louisiana, Oklahoma, and Arkansas, and spending time in Dallas. In the last two weeks of February, he traveled 1,397 miles.

By March, he was in touch with the US Bureau of Investigation, which shared what it had learned from more than a year of tracking the pair. Together, they found Clyde and Bonnie's hideouts and makeshift shooting ranges. Hamer also made contact with Sheriff Schmid and began to work with Deputy Sheriff Bob Alcorn, who had been chasing the couple for months. The former Ranger began to zero in on Louisiana, a state where Clyde wasn't yet accused of a serious crime.

Hamer was so confident in his skills that he fully expected to take Clyde and Bonnie alive. All he had to do, he figured, was find them both sleeping. "It would have been simple to tap each one on the head, kick their weapons out of reach, and handcuff them before they knew what it was all about," he said later.

Really, he should have known better. Catching the elusive couple would, of course, require much more than that.

MAJOR JOSEPH CROWSON, 1900–1934

Major Joseph Crowson.

To Joe Palmer and some other prisoners at Eastham, Major Crowson was a cruel guard, one who was quick to strike inmates and who had once given Palmer a vicious beating. On the morning of January 16, Palmer later testified, he shot Crowson in revenge for "mistreatment to convicts."

Others, however, don't remember him as especially mean.

Crowson grew up near Eastham and started out as a barber in nearby Lovelady. Like several relatives, he ended up working at the prison, living with his parents, Belle and Walter, when he wasn't on duty.

After the escape, prison general manager Lee Simmons criticized Crowson for leaving his post. As the long-arm man, he was supposed to stay on the perimeter, away from others, no matter what. But that day, when Raymond changed work squads, Crowson forgot his orders.

Still, Simmons promised a dying Crowson that he wouldn't let Palmer and Raymond Hamilton get away with the murder.

16

GRAPEVINE, TEX., APRIL 1, 1934.—

---◦---

They don't think they're too smart or desperate,
They know that the law always wins;
  They've been shot at before,
  But they do not ignore
That death is the wages of sin.

—Bonnie Parker, "The Story of Bonnie and Clyde"

WHATEVER ELSE Clyde and Bonnie were feeling in the spring of 1934, they must have been feeling homesick. Cumie Barrow marked the dates of their visits on the wall of her modest Eagle Ford Road home, and she recorded seven or eight meetings between February 13 and late March.

The outlaws were planning another family gathering on Easter Sunday, which fell on April 1. Bonnie had a special surprise for her mother, a white rabbit she had named Sonny Boy.

On a beautiful spring day, the couple parked on a hill near Grapevine, Texas, about a hundred yards from a state highway, while they waited for family members to make the thirty-mile trip northwest. Only one Eastham escapee was still with

A Henry Methvin mugshot, date unknown.

them: Henry Methvin, a Louisiana native who was just short of his twenty-second birthday.

Henry kept watch and enjoyed some whiskey while Clyde took a nap in the backseat of the car. Bonnie played with the rabbit in the front seat.

Around 3:30 P.M., two young state highway patrol officers on motorcycles saw the parked car and rode toward it to see if the occupants needed help.

Bonnie alerted Clyde, who quickly concluded that the officers didn't seem to suspect trouble. "Let's take 'em," he said to Methvin.

Barrow family members contend that Clyde only intended to disarm them and perhaps kidnap them, as he had several other officers. But that's not what Methvin heard.

He raised his gun and took aim at the well-meaning lawmen.

One of the officers fell right away. The other reached for the shotgun shells in his pocket. But before he could load his weapon, either Methvin or Clyde shot him as well. It was a brutal, unprovoked attack.

Mr. and Mrs. Fred Giggal had been enjoying a Sunday outing when they saw the officers turn down the dirt road and then heard a noise like a car backfiring. They drove back toward the loud sound and saw two men. The taller one, they recalled, walked over to one of the fallen officers and shot again, and then both men hurried to their car. Neither Giggal remembered seeing a woman, but they did see the men speed toward them.

"I screamed at my husband to hurry—that they knew we had seen the shooting and would kill us," Mrs. Giggal remembered later that day. Then, just as quickly, the outlaws' car veered off in another direction.

Another witness had a different story. William Schieffer, whose farm was nearby, was on his front porch about four hundred yards away. He said he saw both a man and a woman in riding pants shoot at the officers. Then the smaller of the two, who he believed was a woman, turned one of the officers over and shot him point-blank in the chest.

Police still didn't know that Methvin was with the couple, and Schieffer's story seemed plausible, given Bonnie's wretched reputation. However, he was watching from far away, and Bonnie wasn't able to wear pants with her leg injuries. But, police said, there was evidence Bonnie was there: a cigar stub was found dented with small teeth marks.

The cold-blooded murder on a holy day shocked and deeply angered the community. Patrolman Edward B. Wheeler was twenty-six years old, a sharpshooter and a married four-year veteran. H. D. Murphy was only twenty-two and was on his first day of patrol duty. He was to be married on April 13 and had already rented "a cozy home where he planned to bring his bride in eleven days."

Instead, she would go to his funeral.

Though the Barrow family would later blame Methvin for the murders, the wrath of the public and police was directed at Clyde and Bonnie—especially Bonnie. Until then, she had mostly been considered a tagalong. But Schieffer's account marked her as an evil, vicious killer as well.

Law enforcement should have known what Bonnie looked like by now. But perhaps because of poor communications or a bad eyewitness account, the US Bureau of Investigation circulated a "Wanted for Murder" memo to peace officers that put her height at five feet five inches, at least five inches taller than anyone described her.

The US Bureau of Investigation and Texas Highway Patrol publicly joined the many other police agencies looking for the pair; orders went out to search any car that might be theirs. Behind the scenes, the state highway patrol also made one of its men, a former Texas Ranger named Manny Gault, available full-time to Frank Hamer.

Dallas sheriff's deputies were ordered to circle the city with shotguns in pursuit of the couple. Clyde Barrow is "not a man, he's an animal," Sheriff Schmid said. "He sleeps in the open like a coyote."

Newspaper cartoonist Jack Patton captured the public's frustration with law enforcement's inability to catch Clyde, April 2, 1934.

But a search and real efforts to

H. D. MURPHY, 1911–1934, AND EDWARD B. WHEELER, 1907–1934

H. D. Murphy (left) and Edward B. Wheeler, Texas highway patrol officers killed on April 1, 1934.

The folks in H. D. Murphy's hometown of Alto were proud of their popular 1931 Alto High School graduate. Many people in the town were barely scraping by, too poor to even afford new shoes. But Murphy seemed to have a promising future as a highway patrol officer.

That ended when he and Edward B. Wheeler were shot down near Grapevine on Easter Sunday 1934. Murphy was mourned in one of the largest funerals ever in Alto. School closed at noon and businesses closed so that people could attend.

In addition to his fiancée, he was survived by his father, four brothers, and three sisters.

Edward B. Wheeler met his wife, Doris, when he pulled her over on a traffic stop for having a burned-out taillight. In truth, she said later, he just wanted her name.

The Wheelers had been married less than two years. There were no survivors benefits, so his widow took a job as a secretary with the highway department in Austin. In time, she became a "petticoat ranger," an undercover investigator who helped find illegal gambling.

Years later, after remarrying, Doris Edwards took offense at the fame of Clyde and Bonnie in popular culture. "It's like we don't even count," she said. "Glorifying these killers insults all of us."

block the roads leading out of Texas didn't get underway until Monday or Tuesday, drawing the ire of local newspapers. "Where was the governor, where were the rangers and where was the state highway commission after two members of its force had been shot down?" asked the *Dallas Dispatch*, which called the Barrow bunch "more merciless than rattlesnakes."

LEGEND HAS IT: A WEDDING DRESS

H. D. Murphy died just days before he and his childhood sweetheart, Marie Tullis, were to marry. In one of the saddest of the Bonnie and Clyde stories, she is said to have worn her wedding dress to his funeral.

But did she?

A long story about Murphy's funeral in their hometown newspaper, the *Alto Herald,* said the couple's "school days brought forth a friendship that ripened into love which was to have ended in marriage." It went on, "Miss Tullis is heartbroken, and her friends are extending sincerest sympathy in the unfortunate condition."

The Alto paper and Dallas and Fort Worth papers mentioned the apartment Murphy had rented. But none of them mention Tullis's dress.

Years later, the story started to appear in other newspapers as fact.

Chris Davis, county judge for Cherokee County, said the story is widely accepted in Alto. Family members believe it is true. Given how tough times were, it probably wasn't a fancy white dress, but a new dress she had bought for her special day.

Even with forces mobilized to find them and more rewards offered, Clyde, Bonnie, and Methvin slipped away.

———◦———

Clyde, Bonnie, and Methvin didn't stay out of sight for long. They emerged less than a week later, on Friday, April 6, in northeast Oklahoma, near the Oklahoma-Kansas-Missouri border that had been a refuge several times before.

They had stopped on the side of a highway to sleep, taking turns watching and snoozing. When the sun came up, a motorist reported the suspicious car to Cal Campbell, a constable in Commerce, Oklahoma.

Campbell and Commerce police chief Percy Boyd—who comprised the entire Commerce police force—approached the car, which was stuck in some mud. Spotting a weapon inside the car, Campbell pulled out his gun. Both officers got off a few shots, sending a couple of bullets through the windshield, close enough for Clyde to hear them buzz by.

Clyde and Methvin added their own rapid gunfire. (Boyd said he believed Bonnie also fired a shotgun.) A bullet caught Campbell in the chest, killing him quickly. Boyd was knocked into the dirt by a round that rippled across his head.

With both officers down, the shooting stopped.

Methvin grabbed Boyd and pushed the bleeding officer into the vehicle. Unable to find help at a nearby farmhouse, Clyde flagged down a truck. Using his rifle for persuasion, he forced the driver to pull the car to freedom.

They took off toward Kansas, with Boyd as their hostage.

Witnesses alerted the county sheriff's office and deputies

tried to follow, but Clyde soon lost them. As the hours ticked by, their fears grew that Boyd had died from his wounds or been killed.

But like the other hostages, Boyd was treated reasonably well, considering the circumstances. He struck up a conversation with Bonnie as she cared for and fed the rabbit, and he gradually won her and Clyde over. At one point, Bonnie cleaned Boyd's wound and bandaged his head and then gave him a fresh shirt and necktie because his was bloody. They offered him a suit, but it was too small.

CAL CAMPBELL, 1873–1934

Cal Campbell, Commerce, Oklahoma, town marshal.

Cal Campbell had lived in Commerce, Oklahoma, for about forty years but never intended to be a police officer.

His wife, Edna, died in 1916, leaving him to raise two sons and five daughters. He helped build the Northeast Oklahoma railroad and worked for the state highway department. But he had lost everything in the Depression.

The job as constable paid only $15 a week, but he took it because "it kept us eating," his son Jim said years later. "The only reason he had the job was because the people liked him."

The shooting was so sudden, Jim Campbell said, that "I'm sure my father didn't know who killed him. He was just going out to help someone."

For a full day and into the early morning hours, Clyde took Boyd on a long ride, looping through eastern Kansas and Oklahoma, sometimes at speeds of ninety miles an hour. Mud and dirt covered the windows.

A couple of times, they stopped for a break, once sending Methvin into a grocery store in Fort Scott, Kansas, for sandwiches and other food.

Commerce police chief Percy Boyd, shortly after Clyde and Bonnie released him.

The group didn't know for sure that Cal Campbell had died until they read it in a newspaper that afternoon. Clyde told Boyd he was "sorry they had to shoot Campbell"—but then he and Bonnie joked about the shooting all afternoon. Clyde told Boyd that they did not kill the Grapevine officers and only learned of the murders from newspapers.

Finally, around midnight, Boyd was released about seven miles from Fort Scott, Kansas. He was back home by seven the next morning, with quite a story to tell. "Barrow and companions have no fear of being captured," Boyd said. "They think they're too smart to be captured."

The outlaws had machine guns and sawed-off shotguns, as well as plenty of ammunition. "He thinks quite a lot of himself," Boyd went on. "Bonnie is a lot like him, but she thinks quite a lot of Barrow, you can tell that."

Both Clyde and Bonnie had messages they wanted shared,

Boyd told federal agents later. "You can tell the officers anything you want to, but be sure you tell them the truth," Boyd said Clyde told him. "We would not have fired a shot if the old man (meaning Cal Campbell) had not come out of his car with his pistol."

Bonnie was especially offended that news accounts said she smoked cigars. She "told me she wanted me to tell her public that she does not smoke cigars," Boyd said, even though there was a photo of her with one. "She is plenty mad about it," he said.

While Boyd was sure he had been with Clyde Barrow and Bonnie Parker, he wasn't certain who the third man was. Boyd assumed it was Raymond Hamilton—which prompted an outcry from Raymond himself.

In a handwritten letter from New Orleans's Lafayette Hotel sent care of Sheriff Schmid and postmarked April 7, Raymond was clear that he had nothing to do with the Oklahoma killing. "I want you to let the public and the whole world know I am not with Clyde Barrow and don't go his speed," he wrote. "I'm a lone man and intend to stay that way."

On April 8, investigators found the Oklahoma car abandoned in Kansas. Inside was a collection of leftovers: two pairs of men's socks; a loaf of sliced bread; chewing tobacco; a Boy Scout flashlight; a *Fort Worth Star-Telegram*; a Shreveport, Louisiana, *Journal*; and a bloodstained blue-and-white-checked necktie. Officers also found a head of cabbage and partially chewed carrots, apparently for the pet rabbit.

———◦———

Playing to the outsized interest in the couple's crime sprees, the *Dallas Evening Journal* interviewed the families again.

"Bonnie's not a killer," insisted her sister, Billie.

On Eagle Ford Road, Cumie and Henry denied that Clyde had killed the two Grapevine police officers but shared an interesting tidbit. Clyde was so concerned about what people thought of him that he was now working on "the true story of his life," and a detective magazine was going to publish it.

"It will be a good story, too," Henry added, "for the boy has been over the road the last few years."

After two especially callous killings in a week and up to a dozen murders in all, law enforcement was doing its best to find Clyde and Bonnie, but it wasn't making much progress. Dallas police and sheriffs circled the Barrow filling station three or four times a day. Various agencies interviewed two of the Eastham escapees who had been arrested to see whether either of them could point lawmen to the couple. The Bureau of Investigation reached out to former girlfriends of Clyde and put a Barrow cousin on the payroll as an informant.

At the Dallas police headquarters, a lieutenant had life-sized stand-ups made out of photographs of the two outlaws. The images were placed in a hall so that officers would know what they looked like—and remember that they were still on the loose.

Raymond Hamilton's brother, Floyd, and his stepfather were arrested one night in West Dallas and taken about three hundred miles away to a tiny jail. There they were held for about two weeks without any charges being filed. Floyd said a deputy Dallas sheriff and an assistant prosecutor offered him $5,000 if he would help capture Clyde.

Even for that sum, Floyd refused. If officers found the couple, they "may have to kill them," he said. If Clyde and Bonnie were captured, he added, "you'd want to execute them."

Either way, "it'd still be murder, so I didn't want nothing to do with it," he said.

In mid-April, the outlaw couple and Methvin returned to Texas for another family visit. Bonnie finally gave the pet rabbit to her mother, with a tongue-in-cheek warning: "Keep him away from the cops," she said. "He's been in two gun battles and he'll land at Huntsville if the law finds out."

Barrow and Parker family members knew the long run of increasingly violent crimes wouldn't end well; they even urged the couple to leave the country and start over. But Clyde and Bonnie had been spending more time in Louisiana, near Methvin's home, and were even beginning to dream about trying to find a permanent hideout near Methvin's family. Little by little, they were growing to trust them.

During the latter part of April, Dallas police finally tapped the Barrows' phone. Over a two-week period, handwritten versions of each conversation held on a phone line shared by the Barrows and their neighbors (known as a party line) were recorded. The sixty-nine-page log included several conversations between Cumie Barrow and Emma Parker and plenty of visits between the families as they worried about "C&B," or "the kids," and Floyd Hamilton's arrest. On at least two occasions, one of them called the local newspapers to see if they had published an "extra" edition, which would indicate major news.

Clyde and Bonnie probably called and dropped by during that time. On April 26, Cumie Barrow asked her daughter Nell to come over, saying, "I've got a big pot full of beans and some cornbread," the family's code for their visits. Later that day, a friend called to report that nearby police had tried to stop a Ford V-8 with a man and a woman in it and had gotten gunfire in return. The next morning, Cumie cut short a call saying, "the Howards are out here in front and I want to see them before they leave."

"The Howards," said a Barrow family member, was also a pseudonym used by Jesse James.

The Barrows and Parkers were right to be careful—and fearful. A small group of officers *was* making progress, slowly and quietly.

During an interview with a Bureau of Investigation agent after his release, Percy Boyd mentioned that the second man in the car during his ordeal had been called "Henry." When he and another witness were shown Methvin's photograph a little later, they identified him as the accomplice.

Within days, Lester Kindell, a Bureau of Investigation agent based in New Orleans, and Henderson Jordan, the sheriff of Bienville Parish, Louisiana, got wind that Methvin's family had recently moved to a remote area in the parish from a more populated area near Shreveport. Informants reported that Henry Methvin's dad, Ivy, and one of his brothers, who lived separately, "had shown signs of unusual and mysterious prosperity" after the move.

A raid on a suspected Barrow hideout in Bienville Parish was scheduled and then canceled when Clyde and Bonnie didn't appear to be there. Still, the plans leaked to the Shreveport newspaper, thanks to a talkative Shreveport lawman. Sometime after that, Sheriff Jordan got a message that Ivy Methvin had something to discuss with him.

First through a middleman, and then on their own, Ivy and his wife, Avie, told Sheriff Jordan that they were terrified of Clyde and Bonnie and they were terribly concerned about their son Henry's safety. They said they feared the outlaws would kill them or that their son would die in a shoot-out between police and the hunted couple. (They may also have worried that they

LEGEND HAS IT:
CLYDE'S CORRESPONDENCE

In the midst of one of his bloodiest months, Clyde Barrow appeared to go on a letter-writing binge.

After the Grapevine killings, an angry and profane letter was sent to *Fort Worth Star-Telegram* owner Amon Carter, threatening him and his reporters for saying Bonnie smoked cigars. The lengthy letter today is believed to be a fake, but it frightened Carter enough that he sought police protection for himself and his family.

Henry Ford received a letter from Clyde on April 13. The fan mail extolled Ford's "dandy" cars. "Even if my business hasn't been strickly legal it don't hurt anything to tell you what a fine car you got in the V-8," said the note, signed "Clyde Champion Barrow."

The handwriting didn't look like Bonnie's and was too neat to be Clyde's. In addition, his family said he wouldn't have signed a letter with his fake middle name. But the Henry Ford Museum notes it was the kind of letter a publicity-seeking criminal might send.

might be in legal trouble, too—or even in danger—because of their son's new friends.)

Sheriff Jordan suggested that Henry could turn himself in. But Ivy Methvin said he believed Clyde and Bonnie might murder them all if Henry did that. Clyde was like "a wolf, suspicious and real smart," he told Jordan.

After Raymond Hamilton's letter from the Lafayette Hotel was published, a typed letter was sent to the Dallas district attorney's office, signed "Clyde," that accused Raymond of the Grapevine killings. A thumbprint was included, supposedly to verify that it came from Clyde.

But this letter is also disputed, at least in part because Clyde and Bonnie didn't have access to a typewriter on the run.

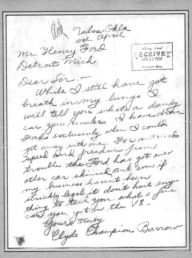

An April 1934 letter allegedly written by Clyde to Henry Ford, in which he shared his appreciation for the powerful V-8.

There is only one letter from Clyde that may be real: a neatly handwritten one sent to Raymond Hamilton when he was in jail that included details about their disagreement over money after the Lancaster bank robbery

That letter was seized and kept by Sheriff Schmid. It sold at auction in June 2017 for $16,250.

Ivy also had an agenda. He wasn't going to help the lawmen simply because he wanted Clyde and Bonnie out of the picture. He wanted Henry's freedom, too. If his family put the couple "on the spot," then his son shouldn't have to finish his jail time or face prosecution for his prison escape or any crimes committed since then.

Ivy Methvin didn't just want a promise—he wanted it in writing from someone official.

After the meeting, Frank Hamer shared the request with Lee Simmons. The Texas prison manager went to Austin to meet with Governor Ferguson and get her consent.

On April 28, law enforcement officials and the Methvins met again. This time, Hamer brought a letter from Simmons making clear that Henry Methvin's Texas sentence would be "wiped out" if the family helped set up Clyde and Bonnie. But the state wouldn't give any assurances about what Henry might have done in Texas after his escape.

It wasn't what the Methvins had hoped for. Ivy, Avie, their two other sons, and Ivy's brother debated the offer at length. Finally, they agreed. They would help the lawmen.

Now they just had to wait for the right moment.

17

NEAR GIBSLAND, LA., MAY 23, 1934.—

Some day they'll go down together;
They'll bury them side by side;
To few it'll be grief—
To the law a relief—
But it's death for Bonnie and Clyde.

—Bonnie Parker, "The Story of Bonnie and Clyde"

IN EARLY May, Clyde and Bonnie slipped into the Dallas area once more. They sat under the spring stars with Emma Parker and shared some recent photographs. Bonnie gave her a poem she had written about her and Clyde's life on the run: "The Story of Bonnie and Clyde."

Death weighed heavily on everyone's mind that evening. Bonnie made her mother promise that she wouldn't say anything ugly about Clyde after they were dead. And the twenty-three-year-old had a special request: she asked her mother to bring her home for one last restful night with her family after her death, rather than leaving her in a funeral home.

As much as it hurt even to think about it, Emma agreed

Clyde and his mother, Cumie, at their family meeting, November 1933.

to her daughter's wishes.

During the same visit, the couple and Henry Methvin drove by the Barrow filling station around midnight looking for Cumie. Only Henry Barrow was there, and he turned over the station to a friend so he could visit with Clyde.

Clyde drove them a couple of miles away to the top of a hill. While Methvin stood lookout, Clyde rifled through his bags and pulled out some papers that looked like legal documents. Henry Barrow later told the *Daily Times Herald* that Clyde said he had purchased a farm in Louisiana for Henry and Cumie and he wanted to complete the paperwork. Calling Methvin's parents "the finest old couple he ever saw," Clyde said that he had moved them to the farm as well.

Despite some digging, Clyde wasn't able to find a pen. He told his father he needed to sign the mysterious documents and bring them back another day.

Henry visited with Clyde and Bonnie until after 1 A.M., when Clyde dropped him off near the filling station. The papers never surfaced again, nor did any evidence of purchased property.

Soon after that, the outlaws showed up in Louisiana for a short visit with Methvin's parents and his brother's family.

Clyde and Bonnie felt comfortable enough to go in the house, taking only their pistols. There, they were able to sleep for four hours. Clyde told the Methvins that it was the first time they had slept in a bed in eight months.

Word of the visits made it to the lawmen pursuing the gang. Special agent Kindell was especially irritated when he heard that his prey had been at the Methvins'. The stopover might have been a great chance to corner the outlaws. But Henry Methvin's brother was worried about his wife and children, Kindell said in a letter to his boss, the Bureau of Investigation director, J. Edgar Hoover.

The Methvins, "while cunning, lack initiative," Kindell wrote. But he was reassured that Clyde and Bonnie were so trusting of the family.

In the same May 14 letter, Kindell spelled out a plan: Frank Hamer would stay in Shreveport or Monroe, the closest cities to the Methvins. Kindell wanted to stay nearby as well. As soon as Henry's father, Ivy, notified Sheriff Jordan of the couple's whereabouts, both Hamer and Kindell would be contacted and would go to wherever Clyde and Bonnie were expected.

Frank Hamer was feeling optimistic, too. In a handwritten letter from the New Inn in Shreveport on May 11, he told the Dallas Bureau of Investigation office that the outlaws might circle back to Dallas soon.

But, he added, "I feel certain we will sack the gang here."

———————o———————

Outrage about the Easter murders had been growing in Dallas, across Texas, and through adjoining states. People were terrified when they heard that Clyde and his crew were sighted—and it was happening more and more.

"Everyone in this country thinks that they see Clyde and Bonnie on every corner and we are trying our best to check all of it," a state highway patrolman wrote in April. "It is some job as most of the officers are scared that they will see them."

Newspapers couldn't write enough about the pair, with stories appearing almost daily in Dallas. Reporters, unaware of Hamer's hiring and the secret work in Louisiana, were increasingly critical that more wasn't being done. A few impatient lawmen took the initiative.

On May 10, four officers swooped into the Barrow filling station in Dallas and asked Cumie Barrow to come with them for an interview.

She had already been called before a Dallas County grand jury investigating whether family members and friends had illegally provided aid to the criminals. But this was different. Instead of stopping in downtown Dallas, three officers continued on with her to the East Texas town of Tyler, about a hundred miles away, quizzing her as they went. Without allowing her a phone call or a lawyer, they took her to a cafeteria for dinner and then to the county jail for the night—her first time in jail.

In the lockup, she saw Billie Parker Mace, Bonnie's sister, who had been arrested earlier in the week. Billie told her that Bonnie's aunt and her brother's wife had also been jailed.

The next morning, they took Cumie to the courthouse for more questioning before returning her to the jail. Then, that evening, they took her home without any further explanation.

Though Cumie thought the men were Texas Rangers, they

turned out to be two highway patrolmen and a deputy sheriff from outside Dallas who had taken matters into their own hands. Among other things, they wanted to know when she had last seen Clyde, if she had seen him on the day of the Easter murders (she hadn't), and if she knew where he hid out (she didn't). They also asked if Clyde would come see her for Mother's Day. He wouldn't, she said.

"They was nice to me all the time," she said later. "I talked to them some, but I didn't tell them anything that would hurt Clyde. They ought to know a mother wouldn't tell nothing on her boy, even if she did know something."

Texas Governor Ferguson lashed out at the intervention, saying that arresting and holding Cumie in another county was "unlawful." Even Frank Hamer's brother, Texas Ranger captain Estill Hamer, was sympathetic. "Those tactics are a mistake," he said. "I do not care how bad the bad man, there isn't any excuse for harassing his mother."

But the troubles for the families weren't over. On Saturday, May 19, Billie Parker Mace was arrested again, this time in Fort Worth. She and Floyd Hamilton, who was already in jail, were charged with the Grapevine murders. William Schieffer, the farmer who lived near where the two highway patrolmen were shot, had been certain a woman had turned over one of the bodies and fired point-blank into it. But he couldn't identify Clyde and Bonnie from mug shots. Instead, he told police, the shooters were Floyd and Billie, based on their photos.

In fact, Floyd and Billie may have been hanging around in the area earlier on that fateful Sunday, though nothing else actually linked them to the murders.

As their families wrestled with more police attention, Clyde and Bonnie were spending more time in northern Louisiana with Henry's kin.

Meanwhile, Frank Hamer and Bienville Parish sheriff Henderson Jordan were growing increasingly edgy about waiting.

At some point, a Methvin family member let Henry know that an arrangement had been made for his freedom in Texas. Saying that he wanted "more than anything in the world to get away from Barrow," Henry promised to try to persuade Clyde and Bonnie to come back to the area soon.

Finally, on the evening of May 21, Henry told his parents he would try to break away from the couple the next day. If they did get separated, Clyde knew that he and Bonnie would find Henry at his parents' home.

The next morning, the three went to Shreveport. Around 9 A.M., Clyde sent Henry into a café to pick up some sandwiches. For some reason, Clyde was distracted by something—possibly a police car—and decided to drive around for a bit.

Seeing Clyde pull away, Henry left the café. He managed to steal a car and make his way to a brother's house by mid-afternoon.

When Clyde and Bonnie couldn't find Henry at the restaurant, they headed to his parents' home, arriving late in the afternoon. Ivy Methvin came out of the house to tell them Henry wasn't there. But, he said, they should come back around 9:15 the next morning.

A few hours later, just after dark, the Methvins let Sheriff Jordan know that Clyde and Bonnie were expected back the next morning.

Jordan was unable to reach Kindell, the Louisiana agent, who was investigating a kidnapping case in another part of the state. But over the next few hours, the posse gathered: Frank Hamer and his partner, Manny Gault, on assignment from the Huntsville prison; Dallas County deputies Bob Alcorn and Ted Hinton; and Jordan and his deputy, Prentiss Oakley. Alcorn, it turned out, was the only one who knew Clyde and what he looked like aside from his now-dated mug shots.

Hamer called Lee Simmons with a message: "The old hen is about ready to hatch; I think the chickens will come off tomorrow."

The group already had picked a good spot along the single road that led to the Methvin's place. On one side was a hill where they could hide in heavy brush and see cars coming from some distance.

Everything finally was falling into place.

In the wee hours of May 23, the six men parked away from the site and took their places, carrying an arsenal of weapons, including shotguns, automatic rifles, and pistols. It was a warm spring night and swarming mosquitos feasted on them in the thick overgrowth. After several hours, their stomachs were rumbling, too.

Around dawn, a nervous Ivy Methvin joined them. Sheriff Jordan had asked Ivy to be there in part so he could keep an eye on him, but also to use him as a decoy. If Clyde was driving as fast as he usually did, he might blow by the officers in a few seconds. But if he saw Henry's father standing by a disabled truck, Clyde likely would stop to see if he needed help. As the sun came up, they jacked up Ivy's truck and removed a tire.

A few cars and the local school bus passed by and offered

to help. Ivy waved them away. As soon as they were gone, the terrified father pleaded with the officers to ditch the whole idea before they all were killed. They sent him back to his post.

While the officers were waiting, Clyde and Bonnie stopped at a local café to pick up breakfast. Clyde was in a short-sleeved shirt and blue pants; his tie hung from the rearview mirror and his coat was folded over the driver's seat. Bonnie had on a red dress and red shoes, and a white tam with a red top was in the car. As they sped toward Ivy Methvin's truck, she was eating a sandwich.

The officers heard the whir of a fast-moving car first. A gray Ford V-8 came quickly into view down the hill, flying thirty or forty miles an hour down a rut-lined road. Even from a hundred yards away, Alcorn knew who it was.

"That's them, boys," he told the others.

———•———

All Clyde saw was Ivy Methvin, standing near his truck. He slowed down to a near stop.

The men on the hill tensed as they aimed their guns.

Suddenly, a logging truck appeared from the opposite direction. To make room for it, Clyde rolled forward.

In the brush, Deputy Prentiss Oakley didn't have time to think. Maybe he felt like Clyde was about to drive off. Or maybe he was overcome with nerves. Whatever the reason, he fired a pair of shots. One hit Clyde in front of his left ear, likely killing him instantly.

Bonnie screamed. "Like a panther," Hamer said later.

For a brief few seconds, there was silence. Then the others

opened fire, sending dozens of bullets into the car and the bodies of the two outlaws. "It was just a roar, a continuous roar, and it kept up for several minutes," Alcorn and Hinton wrote later.

As Clyde's foot came off the pedal, the car rolled into a ditch.

Worried that they were still alive, Alcorn said that he came down from the hill and fired more shots through the back window and Bonnie's side of the car.

By then, they were most definitely dead. Part of Clyde's skull was blown off, as was part of Bonnie's right hand. The scene was ghastly. Bits of blood and tissue dotted the car's interior. Clyde's head hung out the window. Bonnie's hung between her legs.

Though both had guns nearby, neither had had a chance to fire. In interviews after the ambush, some of the lawmen said that they had yelled "Halt" or given the couple a chance to surrender. But in truth, they didn't have time to shout a warning before Oakley started shooting.

As the smoke cleared, Ivy Methvin took off. (The men in the logging truck had run off as soon as the first shots were fired.) Ted Hinton pulled out a 16mm movie camera and began filming, zooming in on the bullet holes that pierced the car door and recording the lifeless bodies. There were weapons in the car, of course: B.A.R.s, shotguns, pistols, gun clips, and at least a thousand rounds of ammunition. The officers also found all the elements of living on the road, including suitcases of clothing, a makeup case, magazines, fifteen license plates, canned food, a saxophone, and some sheet music.

Oakley, Jordan, Hinton, and Hamer went into nearby towns to summon the coroner, get a tow truck, and make important

LEGEND HAS IT:
WAS BONNIE PREGNANT?

As law enforcement got closer to catching up with Clyde and Bonnie, they began to hear that Bonnie was pregnant.

The story may have started with Jimmy Mullins, the former inmate who had helped with the Eastham prison break. He told investigators in an interview that Mary O'Dare, Raymond Hamilton's girlfriend, told him Bonnie was about six months along. There was also a rumor that Bonnie had sought prenatal care south of Dallas, where Clyde grew up. Bonnie also supposedly told a Methvin relative that she was expecting.

Frank Hamer believed the story, noting in a May 11 letter to the Dallas Bureau of Investigation office that Bonnie "is in a delicate condition."

After Bonnie was killed, the coroner didn't mention a pregnancy. Family members say that before she met Clyde, Bonnie had some kind of surgery or medical procedure that left her unable to bear children.

Clyde may have been infertile as well, the result of a virus or other illness that ran through his family. Of the seven children of Cumie and Henry Barrow, only two had biological children.

Still, the story persisted and the debate continues.

phone calls from a local gas station. Hamer let Simmons know the job was done.

Hinton called Sheriff Schmid. "Did you sleep good last night?" he asked his boss.

"No, I didn't," the sheriff replied.

"Well," Hinton said, "you can go on home and sleep now. We just killed 'em both."

By the time the officers returned to the ambush site, locals who had heard the gunshots or the fast-flying rumors were converging on the scene. Once there, they grabbed any kind of souvenir that would connect them to the legend of the notorious killers. They tried to pry away pieces of window glass and steal snippets of clothing and hair. Others scoured for bullets and shotgun shells. Finally, about two hours after the shooting, a tow truck began pulling the pocked car and its bloody inhabitants to a coroner in Arcadia, Louisiana, roughly ten miles away. A caravan of about a hundred and fifty cars followed. Thousands more people were already gathering in Arcadia for a glimpse of the carnage.

On the way, the truck passed the Gibsland, Louisiana, school. Students poured out into the street to see it, forcing the truck to stop—or maybe the sheriff stopped it to make a point. Clyde and Bonnie had been covered with a blanket by then, but one of the students, Mildred Cole Lyons, remembered noticing how tiny Bonnie was.

Lyons went around to the other side and poked her head into the shot-out window. Someone yanked the blanket and Clyde's bloody face, mouth open, came into view. "It was just gruesome," she recalled.

In Arcadia, the bodies were put on stretchers and pushed through the expanding throng to the back of Conger's furniture store, which doubled as a funeral home. The bullet-riddled car was locked behind a fence to keep curiosity seekers away.

The coroner noted more than two dozen bullet holes in each

The men who ambushed Clyde and Bonnie, May 23, 1934: (front row, left to right) Dallas deputy sheriff Bob Alcorn, Bienville Parish sheriff Henderson Jordan, former Texas Ranger Frank Hamer; (back row, left to right) Dallas deputy sheriff Ted Hinton, former Texas Ranger Manny Gault, and Bienville Parish chief deputy Prentiss Oakley.

body, which made embalming challenging. Dillard Darby, who Bonnie had asked to embalm her during his kidnapping a year earlier, actually was called in for assistance.

The room was hot and the smells made it uncomfortable as the coroner recorded their many wounds, cuts, and scars, as well as tattoos and Bonnie's jewelry. She was still wearing her wedding ring from Roy Thornton, as well as two diamond rings, a small watch, and a cross around her neck.

On the other side of the wall, a raucous and growing mob made the work more stressful. Eager to view the deceased, some five hundred people crammed into the furniture store, ripping a door off its hinges and climbing on the new furniture, causing an estimated $1,000 in damage. According to one account, the coroners sprayed embalming fluid to keep them back. People filled the streets outside.

Finally, the paperwork was done and the bodies were covered with white sheets up to their necks. They were moved to the furniture store, where curiosity seekers paraded by them for several hours.

As the bodies were being tended to, the six men who fired the shots gave interviews. They had managed to coordinate an ambush—nearly all of them had played a meaningful role—but they hadn't coordinated their stories. Sheriff Jordan mentioned that they had acted on a tip. Ted Hinton and Bob Alcorn told the *Dallas Dispatch* that they waited two days and nights on the side of the road, though everyone else said they had been there only one night.

Frank Hamer said that he had cleverly set a trap as Clyde was going to pick up mail from a hidden spot on the side of a road, unaided by any tipster. Through other sources, however, the press quickly learned that the Methvins were involved in setting the couple up. (Later, FBI documents and trial testimony clearly spelled out their participation. In August, Henry Methvin received a conditional pardon from Governor Ferguson and

Smoot Schmid (at left, wearing tie) stands next to the bullet-riddled car that Clyde was driving when he and Bonnie were killed, May 23, 1934.

was never tried for the murders of the two highway patrolmen near Grapevine.)

As a result of the ambush, Hamer would further enhance his own reputation as a legendary lawman, especially after interviews in which he took much of the credit for leading the chase and engineering the couple's death.

A posse member reenacts the ambush, showing where the men hid as they waited for the couple to drive by, May 23, 1934.

"I can tell you what happened this morning," Hamer told a St. Louis reporter. "We just shot the devil out of them, that's all."

The hardest part was killing Bonnie, he said. He justified it because, he believed, she shot a highway patrolman at point-blank range.

"I hate to bust a cap on a woman," Hamer said, "especially when she was sitting down. However, if it hadn't been her, it would have been us."

And he insisted on getting in a further dig at her reputation. Though she vehemently denied she smoked cigars (as did others who knew her), Hamer told reporters, "Her love of cigars was fact and not fiction." He knew this, he said, because a gas-station attendant told him so, although she had cigarettes, not cigars, in her lap when she was killed.

In the aftermath of their deaths, even more Bonnie and Clyde legends would take root.

18

DALLAS, TEX.—

———◦———

Here Is Story of Bonnie and Clyde
Penned by Gungirl Before She Died,
Asking for Burial—Side by Side

—*Daily Times Herald* headline over
"The Story of Bonnie and Clyde," May 23, 1934

THEY WOULD not be buried side by side.

Emma Parker wouldn't hear of it.

Readers first learned of Bonnie's burial wish when her poem, which became known as "The Story of Bonnie and Clyde," appeared in Dallas's *Daily Times Herald* after her death. Because Bonnie was always considered part of the Barrow gang during her lifetime, the poem was the first time she got top billing—although eventually that's how the couple would be known.

Emma Parker told reporters soon after her daughter's death that she would not permit the two to be buried together. She had never been enamored with the relationship and blamed Clyde for Bonnie's troubles.

"Clyde had her for two years. Look what he did to her," she said. "Now she's mine. Nobody else has a right to her."

Emma, who had fainted when a reporter told her that Bonnie was dead, couldn't grant Bonnie's wish to spend one final night at home because there was no way to control the flood of curiosity seekers. Crowds jammed the outside of both funeral homes before the bodies arrived Thursday morning, and police had to be called in to maintain order.

By Thursday afternoon, close to 10,000 people packed the front of the Sparkman-Holtz-Brand funeral home near downtown Dallas, clamoring to see Clyde's remains. "They shouted, they stormed, they cajoled," reported the *Dallas Evening Journal.* "Then, they threatened and when this brought no results, began pulling up flowers and shrubbery by the roots and throwing them high into the air."

Police were called again, but there weren't enough of them to control the crowd.

Finally, Henry Barrow agreed to let the public view Clyde's body, which had been dressed in a light gray suit. When the doors opened, hundreds of people pushed through. After hearing some onlookers remark that they were glad Clyde was dead, Henry asked that the doors be closed again. By then, the floors

Crowds gather outside the Sparkman-Holtz-Brand Funeral Home in downtown Dallas, where Clyde's body was taken before his funeral, May 1934.

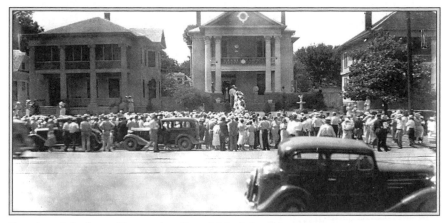

Crowds mob the funeral home where Bonnie's body lay, May 1934.

were scuffed and dirty, the rugs were in a heap, and cigarette butts littered the funeral home's interior.

Across town, a similar scene was playing out at the McKamy-Campbell Funeral Home, where another 20,000 people hoped to get a glimpse of Bonnie, who was dressed in a silky blue dress. There, the mob trampled the lawn and knocked down a fence. The doors were also opened to the public, and up to 5,000 people an hour walked through, destroying expensive carpets.

The scenes replayed on Friday, until an estimated 50,000 people had viewed the outlaws who had stirred up so much fear and fascination.

Clyde Chestnut Barrow, twenty-five years old, was buried Friday evening in a short, private funeral, with family and West Dallas friends attending. Reverend Clifford Andrews, a pastor who ministered to jail prisoners on Sundays, officiated, saying that while he never met Clyde, the Lord loved him and the reverend loved him as well. He noted that according to Clyde's former partner Raymond Hamilton, Clyde often prayed.

During the service, a wreath of flowers was dropped from

a small airplane, a gift from Benny Binion, who ran a local gambling operation.

Reverend Andrews also presided over the private funeral of twenty-three-year-old Bonnie Parker on Saturday afternoon. Officials finally had allowed Billie to leave jail and she joined more than one hundred fifty people who gathered to say good-bye to her sister. The biggest floral arrangement was sent by local newsboys, who had seen sales skyrocket after the couple was killed.

The minister again mentioned the couple's habit of prayer and refused to pass judgment on her. "I pray God to have mercy on her soul," he said.

Emma Parker fainted as her daughter's body was lowered into the grave.

As expected, Clyde and Buck shared a gravestone, with the epitaph, "Gone but not forgotten."

Bonnie's family was more effusive, choosing a rhyme that Billie said reminded them of how she used to be: "As the flowers are all made sweeter by the sunshine and the dew, so this old world is made brighter by the lives of folks like you."

With most criminals, the story would end here, with them forever in their graves. But the interest in Bonnie and Clyde was far from over.

———————

The week after the funerals was eventful for both the Parker and Barrow families.

By the end of May, ballistics tests on the weapons found in Clyde and Bonnie's car showed that some of those guns had been used to kill the two highway patrolmen near Grapevine on Easter Sunday. A judge not only dropped the murder charges against Bonnie's sister, Billie, and Floyd Hamilton, Raymond's brother, but he also apologized to Billie, saying she had "been wronged," and "the law made a mistake."

Both Emma Parker and Cumie Barrow were grieving. Shortly before her son died, Cumie said she had prayed "that I might see him alive again, just once more." She tried to take comfort in knowing their death was quick. But it saddened her to think of them dying on "a lonely country road," so outnumbered, with "shot after shot pouring into them until they were only human wreckage."

Their grief was compounded by a new film advertised only days after their deaths. Apparently using Ted Hinton's footage, the movie showed the damaged car and its gory contents at the ambush site, as well as other moments in the couple's criminal history. "The Most Sensational Film Ever Made," promised the ad for the Majestic Theatre.

Barely a week after their deaths, Cumie barged into the theater while the film was showing, yelling, "You can't do that to my boy."

Employees removed her, but that didn't calm her. She ripped away a photo of Clyde and Bonnie from the theater's display. Police took her to headquarters, where she apologized and was released.

The next day, she and Emma sued to stop the theaters from showing the film, saying it was causing humiliation and embarrassment to family members who had never been in trouble. After some wrangling, the theaters ended the movie's run.

Clyde and Bonnie were out of the daily news now, but their

time on the run was still great fodder for popular monthly detective magazines, which took advantage of their fame, embellishing and distorting their crimes to sell more issues. The so-called pulps also capitalized on a shift in attitudes, thanks to President Roosevelt's war on crime. Outlaws lost popularity and the reputation of police improved.

For instance, the May 1934 issue of *Startling Detective Adventures*, which hit newsstands in April before the couple died, featured the first of a two-part W. D. Jones tell-all, titled, "I Saw Clyde Barrow Kill Five Men."

Touted as "one of the most amazing and thrilling human documents of the year," the stories were allegedly written "as told to" a top editor of the *Dallas Dispatch*. In truth, they appear to be nothing more than an embroidered and exaggerated version of the long statement W. D. had given police in late 1933.

Clyde, according to the first story, "is without doubt the most dangerous criminal in the country today. He kills from pure savagery." He was so awful, W. D. supposedly said, "I believe he would shoot his mother if she got in his way."

Bonnie, the story went on, was "the cigar-smoking, poetry-writing gun girl who rides the death trail with Barrow." (W. D., in interviews years later, was clear that Bonnie did not smoke cigars, and was much less critical of Clyde.)

Another 1934 magazine serial, "The Inside Story of 'Bonnie' Parker and 'The Bloody Barrows,'" ran for six months in *True Detective Mysteries*. The first five stories were supposedly by Ed Portley, chief of detectives in Joplin, Missouri, "as told to C. F. Waers." The last one was allegedly by Sheriff Henderson Jordan of Bienville Parish, Louisiana, as told to Waers. Though some of the details in the six stories were true, many were not. The first installment used stereotypical descriptions to imply Clyde and Bonnie were homosexual, which in the 1930s was considered abnormal or deviant behavior.

"They were a couple that attracted attention," the story said. "Clyde with his small size, his weak chin, his soft hazel eyes, and wavy brown hair, seemed effeminate. In contrast, the woman liked to wear masculine clothes, her mouth was hard, her hair a striking yellow, and she habitually smoked big black cigars."

Other publications painted Bonnie as oversexed or known to the vice squad, suggesting she had once engaged in prostitution.

In August 1934, Emma Parker and Nell Barrow Cowan's error-ridden, romanticized book *Fugitives: The Story of Clyde Barrow and Bonnie Parker, As Told by Bonnie's Mother (Mrs. Emma Parker) and Clyde's Sister (Nell Barrow Cowan)* was published. The foreword states that *Fugitives* isn't intended to glamorize Clyde and Bonnie's behavior, saying that their lives are "the greatest indictment known to modern times against a life of crime." But while acknowledging robberies, murders, and kidnappings, the book also takes pain to humanize them and make excuses for some very serious crimes.

All of the publications increased the intrigue around Clyde and Bonnie and their lives, as did a final act by the US government.

At the end of January 1935, twenty-three people with ties to Clyde, Bonnie, or Raymond Hamilton were charged with harboring or assisting the criminals, including Cumie Barrow; her children Marie and L. C.; Emma Parker; her daughter Billie; W. D. Jones; Henry Methvin; Floyd and Raymond Hamilton;

and their mother and stepfather. At the time, it was one of the largest indictments of its kind in the United States.

Henry Barrow wasn't charged, nor was Clyde's sister Nell.

Clyde O. Eastus, US attorney for the Northern District of Texas, said the indictments were "highly important in the drive to stamp out crime and banditry," and noted that some police officers had died because the accused had helped the couple evade the law.

The case went to trial just three weeks later. On Friday, February 22, newspaper and newsreel photographers were allowed to set up cameras before 10 A.M. to record the accused. The women entered first, shielding their faces with their handbags

Female defendants, some covering their faces, during the February 1935 harboring trial.

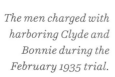

The men charged with harboring Clyde and Bonnie during the February 1935 trial.

and handkerchiefs. The men, who had been chained by the neck and legs on the way there, followed.

Over three days, a jury heard details of Clyde and Bonnie's final year. Jimmy Mullins testified at length about the Eastham prison break. Billie Parker Mace told how she had nursed her sister after she was badly burned.

The star witness was Cumie Barrow. Gray-haired and bent over, the sixty-year-old claimed she visited with Clyde but didn't bring him food, clothing, or guns. "He was my boy. I loved him," she said. And she kept up the secret meetings because "I never knew whether it would be the last time I would see him."

She said that she begged Clyde to give up several times.

She also defended her son L. C., saying that he mostly took her to get togethers because she didn't drive.

Under cross-examination, Eastus asked her why she didn't aid the officers who were looking for Clyde. "I couldn't, he was my boy," she replied.

With that, Eastus shook a Browning automatic rifle in her face. "Did Clyde ever show you one of these?" he asked.

In closing arguments, Cumie's lawyer argued that she should be acquitted, saying, "The Constitution never intended making it a crime for a mother to go see her son."

Eastus retorted angrily: "She is the ringleader."

Henry and Cumie Barrow with their daughter Marie, 1936.

Ultimately, five of the accused pled guilty and the jury found fifteen others guilty as well. (Charges were dismissed against two women for lack of evidence. Raymond Hamilton wasn't tried because he had escaped from prison again and was on the run.) The judge sentenced them quickly, giving Cumie, Emma Parker, and the Hamiltons' mother thirty days in jail. Billie, Mary O'Dare, and Blanche Barrow each got a year and a day. The men got from sixty days to two years, including fifteen months for Methvin and two years for W. D. Jones, which was in addition to his conviction for participating in the crimes. Clyde's little sister, Marie, who was sixteen, was sentenced to an hour in custody.

When Raymond Hamilton was finally caught in April 1935, his punishment was much more severe. Both he and Joe Palmer had been sentenced to death for the murder of Major Crowson during the Eastham breakout, and the state of Texas wasn't going to waste any time delivering their punishment.

Just after midnight on May 10, 1935, Palmer, thirty-two years old, was executed in Old Sparky, the Texas electric chair. A few minutes later, Raymond was brought in. Just shy of his twenty-second birthday, he was wearing a brown jacket and blue silk shirt. He was given a chance to make a final statement, and then his arms and legs were strapped to the tall wooden chair. Copper electrodes were attached to him. A mask covered his face. As witnesses and a newspaper reporter watched, a state official pulled a lever. At 12:27 A.M., Raymond was dead.

It was the ending Clyde Barrow had done everything he could to avoid.

LEGEND HAS IT: MISSING MONEY

According to a story told by Clyde's sister Marie, Henry Barrow saw something else in the car the last time he was with Clyde late one night in early May 1934. As Clyde rifled through a suitcase looking for some papers, Henry was sure he also saw a stack of cash in the luggage.

It wasn't clear where the cash had come from. But after Clyde's death, an unusual story came to light: three men in jail in Fort Worth had offered to pay Clyde $6,000 each to bust them out. Officials there had heard about the plan and stationed extra security at the jail. Some think it is possible Clyde received a down payment on the jailbreak.

After the ambush, however, there was no mention of the suitcase or a large amount of cash. Authorities said they found $500 in Clyde's possession, but nothing else.

Some Barrow family members believe Sheriff Jordan kept the cash.

But there's another version to the story: Years later, Artie Barrow Keys, Clyde's oldest sister, told a reporter that she believed Clyde and Bonnie had buried thousands of dollars in cash on a stretch of road out in a rural part of Dallas. On that last meeting in May, she said, Clyde started to draw a map for his father, but he got distracted and never finished it.

The cash was never reported to be found.

19

HOLLYWOOD, CALIF.—

————o————

You've read the story of Jesse James—
Of how he lived and died;
   If you're still in need
   Of something to read
Here's the story of Bonnie and Clyde.

—Bonnie Parker, "The Story of Bonnie and Clyde"

STORIES CHANGE. Sometimes they change in the retelling. Sometimes they change because the world around us changes. And sometimes they change because other storytellers use them for their own purposes.

So it has been with Clyde and Bonnie.

In the late 1930s, J. Edgar Hoover, as director of the Federal Bureau of Investigation, set out to change the perception of outlaws like Clyde and Bonnie and John Dillinger, the Chicago bank robber. Hoover was disgusted that little boys were playing at being gun-wielding bandits, and he wanted to expose what he saw as the cowardly nature of the criminals.

"I'm going to tell the truth about these rats," he said in the foreword to his 1938 book on the Depression-era bad guys,

Persons in Hiding. "I'm going to tell the truth about their dirty, filthy diseased women."

A 1939 film version of *Persons in Hiding* portrayed the Bonnie-based character as an attractive and greedy woman who falls in love with a second-rate crook. Eager to have more glamour (and more fine perfume) in her life, she is the reason her husband commits bigger and bigger crimes. There was a moral, of course: crime doesn't pay.

That wasn't the first film based on Bonnie and Clyde, though. The 1937 melodrama, *You Only Live Once*, was a much more sympathetic retelling, starring Henry Fonda and Sylvia Sidney as a good couple turned bad by an unfair justice system.

In the 1950s, seductive, troublesome women became more popular lead characters, which created a new opportunity for stories drawn from the West Dallas couple. In these renditions, Bonnie-like women were the masterminds of all the criminal activity. In a mid-1950s article in the men's magazine *Argosy*, titled "Killer in Skirts," Bonnie is portrayed as a dimpled, cigar-chomping hottie who is "America's deadliest sweetheart," a woman who loves her submachine gun almost as much as she loves Clyde.

Two other movies from the era took the same tack. In one, *Gun Crazy*, a sharpshooting woman uses her sex appeal to charm her marksman lover into a life of violent crime. And in *The Bonnie Parker Story*, the gun girl Bonnie goes on a violent crime spree with her sidekick, Guy Darrow.

The Barrow and Parker families seemed to ignore all the retellings, but the public continued to be fascinated by an otherwise ordinary couple gone rotten. Even though the movies weren't huge hits, they found an audience and continued to be shown and reshown on television.

In 1963, John Toland, a historian and author, set out to tell the full story about John Dillinger and his era. In his book *The Dillinger Days*, Toland wove in a few other 1930s outlaws operating at the same time, including Clyde Barrow and Baby Face Nelson. While Toland conducted extensive research and numerous interviews about Dillinger, his Bonnie and Clyde sections relied heavily on the fact-challenged *True Detective Mysteries* series, right down to describing Clyde's "weak chin" and "soft hazel eyes." Toland also stretched beyond the detective magazines, writing that Clyde "had homosexual tendencies."

Two young editors at *Esquire* magazine read Toland's account not as history but as a metaphor for their generation. Robert Benton and David Newman both shared a fondness for French movies and true-crime stories. They were intrigued with Toland's Clyde and Bonnie, and especially with Bonnie's poems, which had been reproduced in the book. They were particularly taken with one line Toland wrote about the pair: "They were, in short, not only outlaws, but outcasts."

Toland meant it as a criticism, suggesting that people looked down on the couple. But Benton and Newman saw the description as a compliment, a reflection of their independence. In 1964 America—a turbulent time of civil rights protests, US involvement in the Vietnam War, and the aftermath of the assassination of President John F. Kennedy—an increasing number of young people saw themselves as outcasts who were misunderstood and out of step with the status quo.

Though the friends had never written a screenplay before,

they were convinced that the couple's antihero story would make a compelling movie that spoke to the sense of alienation that these young adults were feeling.

It helped that Benton was familiar with the outlaws. He had been born in Dallas just two years before Clyde was killed, and had grown up there and in Waxahachie, Texas, not far from where Clyde had spent his childhood.

"Everybody in Texas grew up with Bonnie and Clyde. My father was at their funeral," Benton said later. "You'd go to a Halloween party as a kid and some boy would always be dressed as Clyde and some girl would be dressed as Bonnie.

"Nobody ever dressed up as Dillinger."

Benton and Newman spent their spare time putting together a rough script, reading true detective stories, and writing to Dallas newspapers and police sources for more details. They hoped to attract a major director.

In their introduction to the script, they explained that Bonnie Parker and Clyde Barrow "were heroes of a kind, for they showed bravery in the face of incredible odds, daring in their free enterprise, and style in their manner. They took a delight, it seemed, in foiling the law—the small town cops, the sheriffs, the justices of the peace."

For a new generation born after World War II, Clyde and Bonnie and their participation in the "underworld" of the 1930s represented something more. "What we now call 'the underground,' what the hip people do and are and feel, stems in great part from that 'underworld,'" the novice screenwriters wrote.

In a 2017 interview, Benton said he came to see the couple "as great romantic figures," who saw themselves in a starry-eyed way, as evidenced by Bonnie's poems and by their fascination with their press coverage. While American films portrayed criminals "essentially as one-dimensional mad dogs," he said, European films in the 1960s had begun to present them as "fully rounded human beings." So he and Newman wanted their film "to try to find their humanity."

Drawing on highbrow films being made in France, the script sought to achieve a new level of art and political commentary with an odd mix of silly humor and shocking bloodshed.

Gradually, their movie idea, now called *Bonnie and Clyde*, began to gain traction. A young, handsome, up-and-coming actor, Warren Beatty, bought the script with a plan to produce and star in it. He gave up part of his acting fee for a percentage of the profits.

Beatty brought in an emerging director, Arthur Penn, who saw a chance to weave issues of social and economic injustice into the romantic and criminal legend.

Beatty convinced Warner Brothers to back the project, though Jack Warner, the studio's seventy-five-year-old leader, was deeply skeptical, seeing the film as nothing more than a rehash of old gangster movies. "Who wants to see the rise and fall of a couple of rats?" he asked.

Beatty and Penn brought in a cast of relative unknowns and outsiders who would later become stars, including Faye Dunaway as Bonnie, Gene Hackman as Buck, and Gene Wilder as the undertaker who was kidnapped. Michael J. Pollard played a made-up character named C. W. Moss, who, for simplicity, was a combination of W. D. Jones, Raymond Hamilton, and Henry Methvin.

The lead cast of Bonnie and Clyde, *from left: Gene Hackman as Buck; Estelle Parsons as Blanche; Warren Beatty as Clyde; Faye Dunaway as Bonnie; and Michael J. Pollard as "C. W.," 1967.*

Filming Bonnie and Clyde *on location in Texas, 1966.*

They shot much of the movie in Texas, in places that looked like they hadn't changed in more than thirty years. To add to the drama, Penn used four cameras and spent four days filming the ambush scene. He had a vision for a "spastic and balletic" conclusion, rather than a lyrical one. The ending had "to do something extraordinary, something that makes them into a legend," he said.

That kind of bloodshed would be new for modern movies. Though television was bringing the horrors of the Vietnam War into living rooms for the first time, on-screen violence was still rare in theaters.

The script took liberties with the facts, leaving out, for instance, that Bonnie was badly burned in a car accident and indicating that Clyde mostly robbed banks. In one funny scene, C. W. Moss parks the getaway car between two other cars to disastrous effect—a true story from Dillinger's gang, not Barrow's. In another, the couple tied up Frank Hamer and taunted him; in truth, Hamer never actually met the pair.

But facts weren't the point. "I don't think the original Bonnie and Clyde are very important"—except that they inspired the script and the movie, the director Penn said when the movie debuted in August 1967 at the Montreal Film Festival.

The audience loved it, laughing, cheering, and applauding with gusto at the end.

But critics, some of whom remembered the original outlaws, hated the movie, especially the violence. "It whips through the saga of the cheapjack bandits as though it were funny instead of sordid and grim," wrote Bosley Crowther, the *New York Times* film critic, after seeing it in the festival—one of three reviews he wrote railing at how the movie glorified two criminals. *TIME* magazine dismissed it as "sheer, tasteless aimlessness."

Joe Morgenstern, a young *Newsweek* critic, watched a private screening with Warren Beatty hovering next to him. While he initially was intrigued with the Depression-era saga, Morgenstern found the killing stomach-turning and concluded the movie was a "squalid shoot-'em for the moron trade."

But after thinking more about it, he invited his then-wife, an actress, to go see the movie in a New York theater. He thought she would like the period costumes and the music.

As they watched, the young audience around them went wild, responding gleefully to the characters. "I felt a cold sweat dripping off my neck," Morgenstern said in an interview. "I knew I'd missed the boat."

He borrowed some paper from his wife and began to take notes. That Monday morning, he walked into his editor's office to gingerly explain why he had a lot more he needed to say about this new movie.

The next week's magazine had a most unusual follow-up under Morgenstern's byline: the previous week's review, he said, was "grossly unfair and regrettably inaccurate. I am sorrier to say I wrote it."

On reflection, he said, because the movie "has the power to enthrall and appall, it is an ideal laboratory for the study of violence"—a subject that was increasingly familiar in a year of devastating race riots and vocal protests against the Vietnam War.

A critic reversing his opinion was so extraordinary that Morgenstern's flip-flop became news itself.

While many audiences embraced the film's rebellious nature, those whose friends and families had been targets of the Barrow gang's violence wanted nothing to do with it. Some parents in Texas and elsewhere forbade their teens to see a movie that seemed to celebrate murderers.

In February 1968, *Bonnie and Clyde* was nominated for ten Academy Awards, including Best Picture and every major acting, writing, and directing category. Warner Brothers finally released the film nationwide and it became a bona fide hit as well as a cultural phenomenon. Ultimately, it brought in $70 million worldwide at the box office (equivalent to $500 million today). It also won two Oscars, for best supporting actress and cinematography, and made and broke careers. The film brought fame to Faye Dunaway and wealth to Beatty. Longtime *New York Times* reviewer Bosley Crowther, however, was reassigned.

Bonnie and Clyde themselves got a relaunch, too. The film made them far more famous than they had ever been in real life, even though the on-screen characters barely resembled the real people. Look-alike actors were used in television and magazine ads to pitch airline travel and cars. The country singer Merle Haggard had a hit with his 1968 single, "The Legend of Bonnie & Clyde," from his album of the same name.

———— ○ ————

Henry and Cumie Barrow and Emma Parker were gone long before the movie. But for the surviving members of the Barrow and Parker families, the film reopened wounds that had never fully healed. When it came out, recalled Buddy Barrow, L. C. Barrow's stepson, "my aunt Artie said, 'We're going to have to go through this all over again.'"

The families had tried for years to avoid the shameful and painful legacy the outlaws had left behind. Marie and L. C., as well as the oldest Barrow son, Jack, all had criminal records and spent time in prison well into the 1940s; only sisters Artie and Nell avoided trouble with police or time behind bars.

Barrow said that when he was growing up, his parents, his grandfather Henry Barrow, and his aunts wouldn't discuss Clyde and Bonnie in front of him. If the conversation did turn to the past, he was shooed out of the room. "My family wanted them to rest in peace," he said.

The peace ended, however, once the movie took off. None of the family members or others who were involved with Bonnie and Clyde were happy that the film manipulated their personal stories for someone else's ambition and profit. Blanche Caldwell Barrow Frasure felt like the award-winning portrayal of her "made me look like a screaming horse's ass." Billie Parker Mace Moon, W. D. Jones, and Frank Hamer's widow were among those who also protested how they or their loved ones were portrayed.

There was a silver lining, of sorts. Bolstered by the Hollywood gloss, interest in the outlaw couple grew. Some of those still living—including Ted Hinton, W. D., Ralph Fults, Floyd Hamilton, Marie Barrow Scoma, and Blanche—became minor celebrities themselves, appearing in television specials and documentaries and, in some cases, collaborating on books that told their stories.

Mementos, guns, and other Bonnie and Clyde artifacts—some owned by family, others by lawmen who were allowed to keep them—soared in value. In 1973, the car in which the couple died sold for $175,000 to a Nevada casino. In 1997, the same casino paid $85,000 for the bloodstained, bullet-ripped shirt Clyde was wearing when he was killed. In 2012, two guns Bonnie and Clyde once owned sold for $504,000, and in 2017, a ring that Clyde gave Bonnie sold for $25,000.

In Gibsland, Louisiana, which has two small Bonnie and Clyde museums, volunteers reenact the ambush every year with a festival and look-alike contests on the weekend closest to May 23. The Dallas Historical Society runs a regular Bonnie and Clyde tour on Memorial Day.

No other movie, miniseries, Broadway musical, or documentary about Bonnie and Clyde has won the kind of acclaim or attention that the 1967 movie did. As interest in the couple has waxed and waned, they have continued to be featured in music. Initially, country music told their story as a tragic one of young people gone bad. More recently, they have shown up in rap and hip-hop. Sometimes the lyrics are about guns or darkly violent murder. But most often, those artists, identifying as outsiders who feel mistreated by police and courts, have portrayed Bonnie and Clyde as kindred outcasts trying to survive, supported by their undying love for each other.

Romanticized or vilified, criticized or admired, Bonnie and Clyde remain legendary—no longer for who they were, but for who we want them to be.

A NOTE ABOUT
"THE STORY OF BONNIE AND CLYDE"

———————◆———————

THERE ARE many versions of Bonnie's poem, "The Story of Bonnie and Clyde," in books, recordings, and online.

It first ran in Dallas's *Daily Times Herald* on the day Bonnie and Clyde were killed. The newspaper said it received the poem several months before, with the understanding that it would run only after their deaths.

This version is from *Fugitives,* the 1934 book that claims to tell the families' story. Compared with the newspaper version, the *Fugitives* version uses contractions (such as "Here's" instead of "Here is"), has different punctuation, and includes a stanza that did not appear in the newspaper, the one starting, "From Irving to West Dallas viaduct." The order of the stanzas and some wording also varies. It isn't known whether Bonnie left behind multiple versions or if others made the changes after her death.

> You've read the story of Jesse James—
> Of how he lived and died;
> > If you're still in need
> > Of something to read
> Here's the story of Bonnie and Clyde.

Now Bonnie and Clyde are the Barrow gang.
I'm sure you all have read
How they rob and steal
And how those who squeal
Are usually found dying or dead.

There's lots of untruths to these write-ups;
They're not so ruthless as that;
Their nature is raw;
They hate all the law—
The stool pigeons, spotters, and rats.

They call them cold-blooded killers;
They say they are heartless and mean;
But I say this with pride,
That I once knew Clyde
When he was honest and upright and clean.

But the laws fooled around,
Kept taking him down
And locking him up in a cell,
Till he said to me,
"I'll never be free,
So I'll meet a few of them in hell."

The road was so dimly lighted;
There were no highway signs to guide;
But they made up their minds
If all roads were blind,
They wouldn't give up till they died.

The road gets dimmer and dimmer;
Sometimes you can hardly see;
      But, it's fight, man to man,
      And do all you can,
For they know they can never be free.

From heart-break some people have suffered;
From weariness some people have died;
      But take it all in all,
      Our troubles are small
Till we get like Bonnie and Clyde.

If a policeman is killed in Dallas,
And they have no clew or guide;
      If they can't find a fiend,
      They just wipe their slate clean
And hang it on Bonnie and Clyde.

There's two crimes committed in America
Not accredited to the Barrow mob;
      They had no hand
      In the kidnap demand,
Nor the Kansas City Depot job.

A newsboy once said to his buddy:
"I wish old Clyde would get jumped;
      In these awful hard times
      We'd make a few dimes
If five or six cops would get bumped."

The police haven't got the report yet,
But Clyde called me up today;
      He said, "Don't start any fight—
      We aren't working nights—
We're joining the NRA."*

From Irving to West Dallas viaduct
Is known as the Great Divide,
      Where the women are kin,
      And the men are men,
And they won't "stool" on Bonnie and Clyde.

If they try to act like citizens
And rent them a nice little flat,
      About the third night
      They're invited to fight
By a sub-gun's rat-tat-tat.

They don't think they're too smart or desperate,
They know that the law always wins;
      They've been shot at before,
      But they do not ignore
That death is the wages of sin.

Some day they'll go down together;
They'll bury them side by side;
      To few it'll be grief—
      To the law a relief—
But it's death for Bonnie and Clyde.

*A reference to the Roosevelt Administration's National Recovery Administration.

WHAT HAPPENED TO . . . ?

———————◆———————

THE BARROWS

Cumie and Henry Barrow, along with Marie; her husband, Joe Bill Francis; and Emma Parker, traveled with Charles Stanley's *Crime Doctor* show sometime in late 1935 or 1936. Appearing at county fairs, along with the car in which Clyde and Bonnie were killed, the family members answered questions and spoke about the evils of crime. But they found the experience stressful and participated for just a short time.

In 1938, an acquaintance who was angry with L. C. and Marie fired a shotgun into the Barrow living quarters. Cumie was hit in the face and lost sight in one eye.

In 1940, she and Henry moved into a new house and had indoor plumbing for the first time. After a short illness, Cumie died in 1942, at age sixty-seven. When she died, three of her children—Jack, L. C., and Marie—were in prison for various crimes.

Henry lived into his eighties, dying in 1957.

The bullet-scarred Ford, known as the Bonnie and Clyde "death car," changed hands several times and is now on display at Whiskey Pete's Hotel and Casino in Primm, Nevada.

Jack Barrow, the eldest Barrow child, stayed out of trouble until 1939, when he was accused of shooting a man in a bar fight. He claimed self-defense but was sentenced to prison. He died in 1947, at fifty-two.

Artie Barrow Keys lived into her eighties, dying in 1981.

Nell Barrow Cowan Francis married three times and died in 1968, at age sixty-three.

L. C. Barrow was in and out of prison for robbery and drug and alcohol issues until the 1950s. But he settled down in later life, becoming a reliable truck driver for many years. He died in 1979, at age sixty-six.

Marie Barrow Francis Scoma, the youngest Barrow, divorced Joe Bill Francis and had various scrapes with the law, spending some time in prison. Later, she married Luke Scoma. As the last surviving child, she sold the family's collection of Clyde's possessions, including the shirt and pants he was wearing when he was killed. In the 1990s, she gave extensive interviews to Jonathan Davis for a book, but rejected his manuscript as too negative. She then worked with Phillip Steele on a book but died in 1999 at age eighty, before it was completed.

Blanche Caldwell Barrow Frasure, Buck's wife, served about five years of her ten-year sentence before being paroled. A year later, she married Eddie Frasure, a construction engineer, and they remained together, without incident, until his death from cancer in 1969. In her later years, she renewed friendships with Artie and Marie Barrow and Bonnie's sister. She died in 1988, at age seventy-seven.

THE PARKERS

Emma Krause Parker died in 1944 at fifty-nine years old.

Buster Parker died in 1964 at fifty-five years old.

Billie Jean Parker Mace Moon married Arthur Moon and chose to go by Jean. She never had more children but raised her brother's daughter, Bonnie Ray Parker. Because of the association to the original Bonnie, Jean Moon changed her niece's name to Rhea Leen. Billie Jean died in 1993 at age eighty.

WEST DALLAS

West Dallas continues to be one of Dallas's poorest neighborhoods. In 2012, however, the Margaret Hunt Hill Bridge opened from downtown to the former Eagle Ford Road, now called Singleton Boulevard. A few trendy restaurants have moved in, prompting the first significant investment in the area in decades.

THE ACCOMPLICES

Ralph Fults at one point faced hundreds of years in prison for numerous crimes. But he changed his ways during his time in a Mississippi state penitentiary in the 1940s and won parole. He married, fathered three children, became a Christian, and found a career as a security guard at a boy's orphanage. In his spare time, he pushed for prison reform, such as separating first-time offenders from hardened criminals, and worked to help former criminals go straight. He died in 1993 at age eighty-two.

W. D. Jones served his prison time and then married and lived quietly in Houston for a number of years. After his wife died in the late 1960s, he became addicted to drugs. In 1974, in his late fifties, he was shot and killed during a disagreement in Houston.

Henry Methvin was pardoned in Texas but was tried in Oklahoma for the death of Cal Campbell. He avoided the death penalty and was paroled in 1942, returning to Louisiana. In 1946, he was arrested for stealing cars. In 1948, at age thirty-six, he was run over by a train and killed.

THE OFFICERS

Bob Alcorn left the sheriff's department in the late 1930s to sell used cars. He died in 1964; he was sixty-six.

Manny Gault rejoined the Texas Rangers in 1937. He died in 1947 at sixty-one.

Frank Hamer, already noted for his long and colorful Texas Ranger service, won somewhat mythic status as the man who stopped Bonnie and Clyde. He died in 1955, at the age of seventy-one. After the movie *Bonnie and Clyde* was released, his family sued the filmmakers for defamation, saying the inaccurate portrayal of him in the movie made him look incompetent. The suit was settled for an undisclosed amount of money.

Ted Hinton trained pilots during World War II and then ran a trucking business and operated a motel in a Dallas suburb. He became friendly with the Barrow family and helped L. C. Barrow become a truck driver. He was the last surviving member of the posse that killed the couple. Just before he died in 1977 at age seventy-three, he coauthored a book, *Ambush: The Real Story of Bonnie and Clyde,* that claimed to tell the true story of the ambush—which disagreed with just about every news account and every other first person account of that day.

Henderson Jordan kept the death car until a court ordered him to return it to the original owner. He died in an automobile accident in 1958 at age sixty-one.

Prentiss Oakley succeeded Henderson Jordan as sheriff of Bienville Parish. He died in 1957 at age fifty-two.

Smoot Schmid served as Dallas County sheriff until he was defeated in a runoff in 1946, and then served for six years on the state's board of pardons and paroles. He died in 1963 at age sixty-five.

KEY DATES

---○---

March 24, 1909 or 1910: Clyde Chestnut Barrow born in Telico, Texas.

October 1, 1910: Bonnie Parker born in Rowena, Texas.

1922: Barrows move to West Dallas.

September 25, 1926: Bonnie marries Roy Thornton.

January 1930: Bonnie Parker meets Clyde Barrow at a friend's house.

February 1930: Clyde is arrested at Bonnie's house.

March 5, 1930: Clyde is sentenced to two years in prison.

March 24, 1930: After an escape attempt, Clyde is sentenced to fourteen years in prison.

October 29, 1931: Prisoner Ed Crowder is killed at Eastham Farm.

February 2, 1932: Clyde is paroled from prison.

April 14, 1932: In Electra, Texas, Sheriff James T. Taylor, J. C. Harris, and A. F. McCormick are kidnapped and released, as is mail carrier W. N. Owens.

April 19, 1932: Bonnie and Ralph Fults are arrested and taken to the Kemp calaboose.

April 30, 1932: John Bucher is killed during the robbery of his Hillsboro store.

June 17, 1932: Bonnie is released from the Kaufman County jail.

August 5, 1932: In Stringtown, Oklahoma, Atoka County under-sheriff Eugene Moore is killed, Sheriff Charles Maxwell is seriously wounded, and Haskell Owens is kidnapped.

August 14, 1932: Deputy Sheriff Joe Johns is kidnapped near Carlsbad, New Mexico.

October 11, 1932: Howard Hall is killed during a grocery store robbery in Sherman, Texas.

December 25, 1932: Doyle Johnson is fatally wounded.

January 6, 1933: Deputy Sheriff Malcolm Davis is killed during a stakeout in West Dallas.

January 26, 1933: Springfield, Missouri, Officer Thomas Persell is kidnapped.

April 13, 1933: Joplin, Missouri, detective Harry McGinnis and constable Wes Harryman die in a shoot-out with the Barrow gang.

April 27, 1933: Dillard Darby and Sophia Stone are kidnapped in Ruston, Louisiana.

June 10, 1933: Near Wellington, Texas, Bonnie is badly burned in a car wreck, and Sheriff George Corry and City Marshal Paul Hardy are kidnapped.

June 23, 1933: Alma, Arkansas, city marshal Henry D. Humphrey is fatally wounded.

July 19, 1933: Buck is shot in the head and Blanche is injured by glass in her eye during a shoot-out with multiple officers near Platte City, Missouri.

July 24, 1933: Buck and Blanche are captured near Dexter, Iowa.

July 29, 1933: Buck dies from his head wound.

September 4, 1933: Blanche is sentenced to ten years in prison.

November 22, 1933: Sheriff Schmid and three deputies unsuccessfully try to ambush Clyde and Bonnie as they meet with family members.

January 16, 1934: Clyde and Bonnie help four inmates escape Eastham Farm. Guard Major Crowson is fatally wounded in the breakout and another guard is injured.

February 1, 1934: Former Texas Ranger Frank Hamer hired to find Clyde and Bonnie.

April 1, 1934: State highway patrolmen H. D. Murphy and Edward Wheeler gunned down near Grapevine, Texas.

April 6, 1934: Cal Campbell is killed, and Percy Boyd is kidnapped in a shoot-out near Commerce, Oklahoma.

May 23, 1934: Clyde and Bonnie are killed near Gibsland, Louisiana.

ACKNOWLEDGMENTS

───────◦───────

As a Dallas native, I had long heard about Bonnie and Clyde and wanted to explore some hometown celebrities. Beyond learning their story, I also wanted to understand why, given their crimes, they were so famous and even celebrated. Would it provide any insight into our culture today?

As so often happens, the research took me down unexpected roadways, into issues like poverty, prison, education, and law enforcement. In probing these, I benefited from some personal reading, especially Bryan Stevenson's eye-opening memoir, *Just Mercy: A Story of Justice and Redemption*. Stevenson, a lawyer, represents people facing the death penalty today. His work, he writes, has taught him "a vital lesson: Each of us is more than the worst thing we've ever done." That was a powerful insight for examining the short lives of a violent couple from West Dallas.

A book like this cannot happen without librarians and archivists willing to brainstorm and dig through materials, or libraries and archives, with their vast troves of old newspapers, magazines, and documents from way back when. I am deeply indebted to the folks in the Dallas History & Archives section at the Dallas Public Library, particularly archives manager Brian Collins, photo guru Misty Maberry, and history detective Adrianne Pierce, as well as Crystal Brooks, Sultana Vest, Priscilla Escobedo, and Brandon Murray.

Outside of Dallas, Dora Nolan of the Hill County Genealogical Society in Hillsboro, Texas, was a huge help in digging up old articles, as were librarians in Houston, Texas; Carlsbad, New Mexico; and Fort Smith, Arkansas; and the Oklahoma and Oregon historical societies. Samantha Dodd helped at the Dallas Historical Society and again at the University of Texas at Arlington. Sandy Rogers at the Texas Prison Museum archives patiently answered many questions.

My high school classmate Wendy Golman got me a spot in the press pen at the Dallas International Film Festival so I could interview Robert Benton. Heather Noel, a journalist and friend, helped me wade through microfilm of Dallas's *Daily Times Herald.*

Buddy Barrow and Jonathan Davis were beyond generous in giving their time and knowledge and in providing photographs. The family of Dallas newspaper cartoonist Jack Patton kindly made his fabulous work available.

Terry Baker, a retired sheriff, and John Slate, city of Dallas archivist, were incredibly helpful, and Chris Davis and Virginia Singletary of Cherokee County, Bob Compton, Dr. Lauren Fine, John McBurney, and Maggie Smith gave special assists. I am also grateful to Paul Schneider, who graciously shared a disk of interviews, recordings, and documents, and John Neal Phillips, who helped with photos.

Everything about this book is better because Polly Holyoke and David Stern read the manuscript and shared wise suggestions, and Patricia Hinton read and proofed a later version with care and thoughtful attention.

This book wouldn't have happened at all without the encouragement of my former agent and Viking gang leader Ken Wright; my unflappable agent, Susan Cohen; and my supportive, patient, and thoughtful editor, Catherine Frank. Jody Corbett and Janet Pascal brought precision and clarity to the words, and Nancy Brennan designed a cover and interior that perfectly capture the outlaws and the times.

Last, I am forever thankful for my "Clyde," Scott McCartney, who listens, reads, cooks, and keeps us moving forward. There is no greater joy than sharing this ride with him.

A NOTE ABOUT FACTS AND SOURCES

———————◦———————

TRUTH IS slippery, especially in stories like this one. As soon as you think you have a grip on it, certainty slides right out of your grasp. With multiple stories of Bonnie and Clyde's crimes, trying to resolve the contradictions and understand how the legends grew was challenging and, in a few cases, impossible.

Was Bonnie burned in a fire or by battery acid? (Some accounts cite a fire, but it was almost certainly battery acid.) Was Clyde born in 1909 or 1910? (Hard to say. Several family members and Cumie's Bible say 1910, but the 1910 Census, taken that April, lists him as a year old, not "1/12," as a month-old infant would have appeared.) Police statements differ from eyewitness reports. Sometimes lore becomes reality.

While this book isn't intended to be a blow-by-blow tell-all, I still had to resolve the conflicting accounts from family members, fellow criminals, and law enforcement, so I sought to get as close to original events and sources as possible. For instance, I used Blanche Barrow's book primarily when it dealt with events where she was present.

Nell Barrow Cowan and Emma Parker's story, *Fugitives*, published in 1934, has been criticized as fictionalized. But it has insights and stories about the families that aren't available anywhere else—including the revelation that Bonnie brought the gun into the Waco jail in 1930. I tried to use it judiciously.

Getting to the closest source meant seeking out local stories and firsthand accounts, since details in those were often very different from wire service reports and hyped-up detective magazines. That meant collecting stacks of original stories from libraries, microfilm, and multiple subscription databases. In addition, some original articles are reproduced in *On the Trail of Bonnie & Clyde, Then and Now.*

The Dallas History & Archives section of the downtown Dallas Public Library had a real treasure: Sheriff Smoot Schmid's carefully preserved scrapbooks, which contained selected articles from four Dallas newspapers neatly pasted into oversized wallpaper sample books.

In addition, I drew on nearly one thousand pages of FBI documents related to Bonnie and Clyde, which were released in 2008. They are hard to read and aren't in chronological order. But they provide dates and facts not available anywhere else.

Other useful documents were at the Texas Prison Museum in Huntsville, the Texas Ranger Hall of Fame and Museum in Waco, Kent Biffle's papers at the University of Texas at Arlington, and Jeff Guinn's papers in the Bonnie and Clyde Research Collection at Stephen F. Austin State University in Nacogdoches, Texas.

I benefitted greatly from the authors who have made this trek before me. John Neal Phillips interviewed many Barrow and Parker family members and friends in the 1980s and 1990s, and his two books, *Running with Bonnie and Clyde: The Ten Fast Years of Ralph Fults*, and his edition of Blanche Barrow's *My Life with Bonnie & Clyde*, are crucial to any dive into the couple's career. Jonathan Davis's extensive 1990s interviews with Marie Barrow Scoma, reflected in his book, *Bonnie & Clyde & Marie: A Sister's Perspective on the Notorious Barrow Gang*, and one with James R. Knight, *Bonnie and Clyde: A Twenty-First Century Update*, also were invaluable.

Guinn's 2009 book, *Go Down Together: The True, Untold Story of Bonnie and Clyde*, is one of the most readable accounts about the couple, and Paul Schneider's 2009 book, *Bonnie and Clyde: The Lives Behind the Legend* is one of the most deeply researched.

The resources listed in the bibliography tie directly to the text and are not comprehensive. If you have any questions about sources, please contact me through my website, karenblumenthal. com, where you will also find a more detailed bibliography.

SOURCE NOTES

———————◆———————

1. JOPLIN, MO., APRIL 1933.—

"You've read the story . . .": Jan I. Fortune, editor. *Fugitives: The Story of Clyde Barrow and Bonnie Parker as Told by Bonnie's Mother (Mrs. Emma Parker) and Clyde's Sister (Nell Barrow Cowan)*, Fort Worth, Texas: Wild Horse Press, 2013, 247.

"Their whole image . . . happy": Jeff Guinn. *Go Down Together: The True, Untold Story of Bonnie & Clyde*, New York: Simon & Schuster, 2009, 176.

"living hell": Fortune. *Fugitives*, 13.

2. TELICO, TEX., MARCH 24, 1909.—

"They call them cold-blooded killers . . .": Fortune, *Fugitives*, 247.

"Everything looked bright and rosey . . . We found that life . . .": Cumie Barrow. Unpublished and unpaged manuscript. Bonnie & Clyde Research Collection, box 2, folder 6, East Texas Research Center, Ralph W. Steen Library, Stephen F. Austin State University.

"a good boy, playful and full of life": ibid.

"He liked music . . .": ibid.

3. WEST OF DALLAS, TEX., 1922.—

"From Irving to West Dallas viaduct . . .": Fortune. *Fugitives*, 249.

"idle farm hands": "Relief for Itinerant Campers to Be Sought at Charities Meeting," *Dallas Morning News*, February 21, 1923.

"some mythological river of death": "City's Sewage Fouls Trinity for 150 Miles," *Dallas Morning News*, September 14, 1929.

"tattered wagons . . .": "Relief for Itinerant Campers . . . ," *Dallas Morning News*, February 21, 1923.

"We have no parks . . .": Helen Bullock. "Of Hattie Rankin Moore, Who Loved West Dallas," *Dallas Morning News*, October 7, 1951.

"You didn't have to . . .": Rena Pederson. "Badmen's Pal 'Outgrowed' Wild Life," *Dallas Morning News*, March 28, 1976.

"He would sometimes . . . wayward women in the neighborhood": Cumie Barrow. Unpublished manuscript.

"Whenever a car was stolen . . .": John Neal Phillips. *Running with Bonnie and Clyde: The Ten Fast Years of Ralph Fults*, Norman, Oklahoma: University of Oklahoma Press, 1996, 46.

"After he was picked up . . .": Cumie Barrow. Unpublished manuscript.

"a beautiful baby . . .": Fortune. *Fugitives*, 47–48.

"I'd tell her, 'Be quiet'. . .": Jud Collins, interviewer. *The Truth About Bonnie and Clyde, as told by Billie Jean Parker (Bonnie's Sister)*, New York: RCA Victor, 1968, album, converted to digital.

"who was having . . .": Fortune. *Fugitives*, 59.

"I wish to tell you . . .": ibid., 62.

"Sure am lonesome": ibid., 63.

"Sure am blue tonight": ibid., 66.

"Bonnie could turn heads": Ted Hinton, as told to Larry Grove. *Ambush: The Real Story of Bonnie and Clyde*, Fredericksburg, Texas: Shoal Creek Publishers, Inc., 1979, xiii.

"with his dark wavy hair . . .": Fortune. *Fugitives*, 71.

"I thought she was going crazy": ibid., 72.

4. WACO, TEX., MARCH 1930.—

"But the laws fooled around . . .": Fortune. *Fugitives*, 248.

"I have had the blues . . .": ibid., 74.

"I was so blue and . . .": ibid., 76.

"Wouldn't that be terrible?": ibid., 78.

"Schoolboy": "Jailers Held Up With Pistol; Prisoners Escape," *Waco News-Tribune*, March 12, 1930.

"Not a fit place . . .": Harry Benge Crozier. "Prison Not Fit for Dog Moody Informs House," *Dallas Morning News*, January 30, 1930.

"worked the town . . .": "Waco's Dumbell Bandits, Captured in Ohio, Back in M'Lennan County Jail," *Waco Sunday Tribune*, March 23, 1930.

"Baby Thugs Captured": "Baby Thugs Captured," *Waco News-Tribune*, March 19, 1930.

"Waco's Dumbell Bandits . . ." and "baby dumbells": "Waco's Dumbell Bandits . . ." *Waco Sunday Tribune*, March 23, 1930.

"I have lost my patience . . .": "'Baby Thugs' Get Long Terms," *Waco Times-Herald*, March 24, 1930.

"I think it would be . . .": ibid.

"Listen, I've got a bunch of bad hombres . . .": "Jail Break Plot Fails," *Waco News-Tribune*, March 27, 1930.

"Horse feathers": "Baby Thug a Killer?" *Waco News-Tribune*, March 29, 1930.

"Clyde was just 18 last Monday. . ." through "appeared amused": "Mrs. Barrow Blames Bad Companions for Downfall of Her 'Baby Thug' Son," *Waco News-Tribune*, March 28, 1930.

"You are the sweetest . . .": Cumie Barrow. Unpublished manuscript.

5. EASTHAM FARM, TEXAS PRISON SYSTEM, 1930–1932.—

"We each of us have a . . .": Fortune. *Fugitives,* 109.

"From this time on. . . .": Lee Simmons. *Assignment Huntsville: Memoirs of a Texas Prison Official*, Austin, Texas: University of Texas Press, 1957, 63.

"inhuman": ibid., ix.

"Gentlemen, it's just . . .": ibid., x.

"they'll bust your head open": John Neal Phillips and Ralph Fults. "The Man Who Ran with Bonnie and Clyde," *Dallas Life Magazine*, June 10, 1984, 10.

"they take you over . . .": Phillips. *Running with Bonnie and Clyde*, 8.

"They ain't supposed to be . . .": ibid., 41.

"eight hour days": ibid., 37.

"Everywhere was filth and garbage": Simmons. *Assignment Huntsville*, 67.

"loved to laugh": Phillips and Fults. "The Man Who Ran . . . ," 11.

"He couldn't stand to see . . .": Bill Muller. "Ex-gangster Only One Left to Tell Tale of Bonnie, Clyde," *Dallas Times Herald*, July 5, 1991.

"little blue-eyed girl": Phillips and Fults. "The Man Who Ran . . . ," 11.

"Therefore, we ask you to recommend . . ." through "support of his mother": Byron C. Utecht. "Many Persons Asked Clemency for Barrow," *Fort Worth Star-Telegram*, January 19, 1934.

"I'm telling you . . .": Harry McCormick. "Nine Texas Convicts Maimed Selves During Year; Inmates of Two Farms," *Houston Press*, undated but appears to be 1935, from the Harry McCormick scrapbook, Dallas Public Library.

"schoolboy to a rattlesnake": Phillips and Fults. "The Man Who Ran . . . ," 11.

6. ELECTRA, TEX., APRIL 14, 1932.—

"If he had returned to me sometime . . .": Fortune. *Fugitives*, 111.

"his dimple and smile working". Ibid., 103.

"I've got to stay close to home": ibid., 105.

"draggin' me downtown" through ". . . kill me": Phillips and Fults. "The Man Who Ran . . . ," 13.

"I gotta take you down": *Ralph Fults Tells His Story with Bonnie and Clyde*. Southwest Historical Inc., courtesy of Paul Schneider.

"they could not afford to go to jail.": "Bandit Trio Kidnaps Three; Two Take Them For Ride," *Electra News*, April 14, 1932.

"Mrs. Owens was frantic with grief": "W. N. Owens Held 12 Hours Thursday by Two Kidnapers," *Electra News*, April 21, 1932.

"bright, refreshing, and pleasant to be with": Phillips and Fults. "The Man Who. Ran . . ." 26.

"I'm just a loser . . .": Phillips. *Running with Bonnie and Clyde*, 80.

"All in all, it was enough . . .": Fortune. *Fugitives*, 107.

"The Story of Suicide Sal" and "Not long ago . . .": ibid., 108–112.

7. STRINGTOWN, OKLA., AUGUST 5, 1932.—

"Now Bonnie and Clyde are the Barrow gang . . .": Fortune. *Fugitives,* 247.

"more quiet and . . ." through ". . . more to do with him": ibid., 119.

"He drove like a devil . . .": Fortune. *Fugitives*, 126.

"There were numerous bullet holes . . .": E.J. Dowd. "Memorandum, re: Clyde Champion Barrow with aliases," US Bureau of Investigation #26-4114-61, FBI records part 5, 1.

"The Chief just stood up . . .": Tom Lachenmayer. *History of the Dallas Police Department*, December 10, 1974, 9.

"Listen over the radio . . .": Fortune. *Fugitives*, 121.

"Where is that money?": "Bandits Leave No Trail After $440 Robbery," *Dallas Morning News,* August 2, 1932.

"I haven't seen him . . ." through "anything in the world": Fortune. *Fugitives*, 121.

"Consider yourselves under arrest": "Atoka County Officers Fall Victims of Bandits Guns at Stringtown, Friday Night," original news story reproduced in the *Atoka Indian Citizen*, June 24, 1992.

"Young women screamed and fainted . . .": Ed Portley, as told to C. F. Waers. "The Inside Story of 'Bonnie' Parker and 'The Bloody Barrows,'" *True Detective Mysteries*, May 1934, 72.

"Car lights shone like meteors . . .": ibid.

"put up such a pitiful story" and "caused me so much worry . . . ": Mamie Redden. Letter to the editor. "More About Barrow, Hamilton, and the Death of Gene Moore," *Atoka County Times*, March 28, 1968.

"he never answered the door at night": Rob Rogers. "A Life Remembered: Brush with Famed Gunman Changed His Life," *News-Review*, Roseburg, Oregon, November 21, 2003.

"definite information": "Man Hunt Gets Hot as Dallas Seeks Gunmen," *Dallas Morning News*, August 9, 1932.

"fight to the death,": "Pair Wanted for Slayings Sought in Texas Holdups," *Daily Times Herald*, August 8, 1932.

"would be accomplished before the end of the week": "Police Expect Early Arrest of 2 Killers," *Daily Times Herald*, August 9, 1932.

EUGENE C. MOORE, 1901–1932, AND SHERIFF CHARLES MAXWELL

"the roughest thing for me was growing up without a father": Mike Royko. *For the Love of Mike: More of the Best of Mike Royko*, Chicago, Illinois: University of Chicago Press, 2001, 205.

8. CARLSBAD, N.MEX., AUGUST 14, 1932.—

"There's lots of untruths to these write-ups . . .": Fortune. *Fugitives,* 247.

"James White" and "Jack Smith": "Local Deputy Sheriff Safe in San Antonio; Desperados Escape," *Daily Current-Argus*, August 15, 1932.

"Whose Ford is this?": Phillips. *Running with Bonnie and Clyde*, 105.

"They told her to shut up . . .": Deputy Sheriff Joe Johns. "Former Eddy County Sheriff Writes Own Complete Story of Wild Ride with Bandits," *Daily Current-Argus*, August 17, 1932.

"I wasn't nervous . . .": ibid.

"Honey": "Deputy Not Slain," *Dallas Morning News*, August 16, 1932.

"You've had just 24 hours of it now. . . .": Johns. "Former Eddy County Sheriff . . ." August 17, 1932.

"You shore have caused us . . .": ibid.

"pretty rough": "Shanghai Sheriff After Gun Fight Over Stolen Car," *Las Vegas (N.M.) Daily Optic*, August 15, 1932.

"Bonnie Parker alias Bonnie . . .": Letter from J. C. Willis, Sheriff, Wharton County, to Chief of Detectives, Identification Bureau, Dallas, Texas, dated August 19, 1932. Dallas Municipal Archives, accessed from Portal to Texas History.

9. SHERMAN, TEX., OCTOBER 11, 1932.—

"If a policeman is killed in Dallas . . .": Fortune. *Fugitives*, 248.

"Mr. and Mrs. Roy Bailey": "Report of Special Agent C.B. Winstead, Dallas, Texas, March 6, 1933," US Bureau of Investigation #26-4114-18, FBI records part 1, 2.

"You can't do that": Winston G. Ramsey, ed. *On the Trail of Bonnie & Clyde, Then and Now*, London: Battle of Britain International Ltd., 2003, 74.

"he admitted so many crimes . . .": Fortune. *Fugitives*, 118.

"We couldn't have done that . . . ": ibid., 141.

"Smoot": "How 'Smoot' Schmid Got His Nickname," *Dallas Morning News*, August 28, 1932.

"Say, don't I know you . . .": Sid Underwood. *Depression Desperado: The Chronicle of Raymond Hamilton*, Austin, Texas.: Eakin Press, 1995, 22.

HOWARD HALL, 1875–1932

"upright Christian life": Ramsey. *On the Trail of Bonnie & Clyde*, 77.

10. TEMPLE, TEX., DECEMBER 25, 1932.—

"From heart-break some people have suffered . . .": Fortune. *Fugitives,* 248.

"Dub," "Deacon," or "W. D.": Phillips. *Running with Bonnie and Clyde* 118 111.

"it seemed sort of big to be out with two famous outlaws": W. D. Jones. "Riding with Bonnie & Clyde," *Playboy*, November 1968. Dallas History & Archives, "Bonnie and Clyde, 1960–1969" folder, Dallas Public Library.

"Boy, you can't go home . . . ": ibid.

"Oh, don't shoot! Think of my babies": "Two Women Charged After Deputy Slain," *Daily Times Herald*, January 7, 1933.

"the officers ambushed themselves": "Many Officers Join Hunt for Deputy Slayers," *Fort Worth Star-Telegram*, January 8, 1933.

"how Clyde had spent a fair slice of his money": Hinton. *Ambush*, 100.

"modern 'Robin Hoods'": "Tight Lips Balk Police Hunt for Dallas Killers," *Dallas Dispatch*, January 15, 1933, Smoot Schmid scrapbooks, January 1933–July 1933 Dallas History & Archives, Dallas Public Library.

"With Jesse James dead . . .": "Pretty Boy Is New Suspect in Killing; Jesse James Next," *Dallas Morning News*, January 20, 1933.

"the girl can handle pistols . . .": "Tough 2-Gun Girl with Desperadoes Who Killed Davis," *Dallas Morning News*, January 13, 1933.

"She is as tough as the back end . . .": ibid.

"We may hear any minute . . ." through ". . . as bad as kill a man": Andrew De Shong, "Mothers of Two West Dallas Outlaws Fearful for Future," *Daily Times Herald*, January 10, 1933.

"We wanted him to live . . .": Fortune. *Fugitives*, 154.

"He slid the shotgun . . .": Kit Brothers. "Policeman Kidnapped by Barrows dies at 81," *Joplin Globe*, July 27, 1989.

MALCOLM DAVIS, 1881–1933

"We are too ready to criticize . . .": "Third Woman Quizzed in Deputy Killing," *Fort Worth Star-Telegram*, January 9, 1933.

11. JOPLIN, MO., APRIL 13, 1933.—

"If they try to act like citizens . . .": Fortune. *Fugitives*, 249.

"There were no lengths . . .": Jonathan Davis. *Bonnie & Clyde & Marie: A Sister's Perspective on the Notorious Barrow Gang*, Nacogdoches, Texas: Stephen F. Austin State University Press, 2014, 99.

"I was glad to cook anything . . .": Blanche Caldwell Barrow, edited by John Neal Phillips. *My Life with Bonnie & Clyde*, Norman, Oklahoma: University of Oklahoma Press, 2004, 40.

"He knocked her across the bedroom . . . ": ibid., 48–49.

"Suicide Sal": Interview with George B. Kahler by Sgt. Charles E. Walker. "To Serve & Protect: A Collection of Memories," Missouri State Highway Patrol, Public Information and Education Division, 2006, 21.

"Just a minute. . . .": Louis E. Eslick. "Report of raid at Thirty-fourth and Oakridge Drive," Missouri State Highway Patrol, April 14, 1933, courtesy of Paul Schneider, 3.

"Get in there as quickly as . . ." and "For God's sake . . .": "Desperados Kill Two Officers Here," *Joplin Globe*, April 14, 1933.

"shoot to kill": "Bullets Await Barrow Boys in Texas," *Daily Times Herald,* April 14, 1933.

"being framed": "Mother Hugs Belief Her Boys Not Killers As Older Sons Hunted," *Dallas Morning News*, April 15, 1933.

"Run, run, run. . . .": Jones. "Running with Bonnie & Clyde," 164.

"Every minute of your life . . ." and "You done slipped up . . . ": Kent Biffle, interview with W. D. Jones. June 1969, cassette transferred to CD, Kent Biffle Papers, box 55, Special Collections, University of Texas at Arlington.

"two women in the same kitchen . . . ": ibid.

"got to liking": Carolyn Carver. "A Day With Bonnie and Clyde," *North Louisiana Historical Association Journal*, Winter 1971.

"I know we're going to get it . . ." and "Clyde didn't see the humor": Frank X. Tolbert. "Taken for a Ride by Bonnie and Clyde," *Dallas Morning News*, March 18, 1968.

"Neither of us is much worse for the experience": H. D. Darby. "Darby Relates Details of His Ride with Kidnapers," *Ruston Daily Leader*, April 28, 1933.

JOHN WESLEY HARRYMAN, 1881–1933, AND HARRY MCGINNIS, 1879–1933

"It wasn't until my brothers and sisters . . .": Mike Royko. *For the Love of Mike*, 205.

"the Irishman.": "M'Ginnis Was Popular As A Peace Officer," *Joplin Globe*, April 15, 1933.

12. WELLINGTON, TEX., JUNE 10, 1933.—

"This road was so dimly lighted . . . ": Fortune. *Fugitives*, 248.

"I begged Buck to stay" and "There isn't a chance in the world": Cumie Barrow. Unpublished manuscript.

"literally shot up the town": "Bandits Raid Lucerne," *Logansport (Ind.) Pharos-Tribune*, May 12, 1933.

"Those who saw the bandits . . .": ibid.

"Bonnie Parker is a gun-woman . . . ": C. B. Winstead memo, US Bureau of Investigation #26-4114-35, May 21, 1933, FBI records part 1, 3.

"Well, have they caught your brothers yet?": Davis. *Bonnie & Clyde & Me*, 113.

"I love him and I'm going . . .": Fortune. *Fugitives*, 174.

"a few hundred dollars" and "we had to laugh to keep from crying": Barrow. *My Life with Bonnie & Clyde*, 80.

"Hold your hats! It might not have a bottom": Jud Collins. *The Truth About Bonnie and Clyde, as told by Billie Jean Parker (Bonnie's Sister)*.

"We can't afford it": Associated Press, "Wellington Officers Say Barrow Pair Abductors," *Amarillo Daily News*, June 12, 1933.

"I thought they were probably a couple of drunks": "Kidnappers of Local Officers Still At Large," *Wellington Leader*, June 15, 1933.

"for all the trouble we've been . . .": "Bonnie and Clyde," Wellington, Texas, website, wellingtontx.com/9578158_88485.htm.

"Are we going to kill those men?": "Barrow Boys Take 2 Officers Captive After Car Crashes," *Dallas Morning News*, June 12, 1933.

"He rolled up to the house . . ." and "was out of her head for days": Marge Crumbaker. "Bonnie, Clyde and 2 Who Remember Them," *Texas Tempo*, May 1968, from the Bonnie and Clyde Research Collection, East Texas Research Center, box 2, folder 39, Ralph W. Steen Library, Stephen F. Austin State University.

HENRY D. HUMPHREY, 1882–1933

"It was hard on all of us": Mike Royko. "The Real Bonnie and Clyde Left a Trail of Lingering Sorrow," *Des Moines Tribune*, February 24, 1968.

13. PLATTE CITY, MO., JULY 19, 1933.—

"Sometimes: Across the fields of yesterday . . .": Barrow. *My Life with Bonnie & Clyde*, 198.

"Line Up": "The Line-Up," *True Detective Mysteries*, May 1938, 72, and September 1933, 69.

"war on crime": Joseph B. Keenan. "Uncle Sam Presses His New War on Crime," *New York Times*, August 20, 1933.

"brought back so many guns . . .": "Shaking With Fear, Prisoner Tells of More Barrow Killings," *Dallas Morning News*, November 26, 1933.

"We didn't see many strangers . . .": Francis Williams. "The Day Bonnie and Clyde Shot It Out With the Law in Ferrelview," *Discover North*, March 1974, 4, from the Bonnie and Clyde Research Collection, box 1, folder 14, East Texas Research Center, Ralph W. Steen Library, Stephen F. Austin State University.

"I'm getting pretty damn tired of . . .": ibid., 6.

"I looked at her . . .": Dorothy Gast. "Bonnie and Clyde No Heroes, Victim Says," *Kansas City Star*, September 17, 1978.

"It was quite a spectacular thing. . . .": ibid.

"unless peace officers are equipped with . . . ": E. J. Dowd. US Bureau of Investigation #26-4114-53, July 8, 1933, FBI records part 1, 6.

"Luck must be with them. . . ." and "Either of them . . .": "Luck of Barrow Boys Can't Last, Former Pal of

Killer Says," *Daily Times Herald,* July 20, 1933, from Schmid scrapbook, July–October 1933, Dallas Public Library.

"They're living on borrowed . . ." and "May God spare my boys": "Barrow Boys' Mother Knows Sons Doomed; Were Here Recently," *Daily Times Herald*, July 23, 1933, from Schmid scrapbook, July–October 1933, Dallas Public Library.

"I noticed he was . . ." and "You missing any . . . ": Robert Hullihan. "When an Iowa Shootin' Fool Met 'Bloody Barrows,' " *Des Moines Register*, October 26, 1975.

"I knew they'd got Clyde. . . .": Fortune. *Fugitives*, 201-202.

"Daddy, Daddy, are you. . . .": Donald Grant. "Posse Plans Attack Today to Seize Trio," *Des Moines Register*, July 25, 1933.

14. DES MOINES, IOWA, JULY 1933.—

"The road gets dimmer and dimmer. . . .": Fortune. *Fugitives*, 248.

"Who else was with you? . . ." through ". . . was the end": "Mrs. Barrow Feared Fight Was 'The End,' " *Des Moines Register*, July 25, 1933.

"I've got to see my . . ." through ". . . who he is": "He's My Boy, Sobs Barrow's Mother; I Want to See Him," *Dallas Morning News*, July 25, 1933.

"You were lucky you got out of my way": Donald Grant. "Trail is Cold in Gang Hunt," *Des Moines Register*, July 26, 1933.

"Even though realizing . . .": D. W. Brantley. US Bureau of Investigation #26-4114-90, August 17, 1933, FBI records part 1, 8.

"Oh darling! My baby . . .": "Mother Hopes Clyde Barrow is Out of State," *Des Moines Register*, July 27, 1933.

"No. I feel that either . . .": ibid.

"Bonnie and Clyde are in love . . ." through ". . . dead wrong": "Barrow and Girl Pal Won't Be Taken Alive, Former Partner Says," *Daily Times Herald*, July 26, 1933.

"it was torment. . . .": Biffle, interview with W. D. Jones.

"I'd had enough blood and hell": Jones. "Riding with Bonnie and Clyde," 165.

"never wanted to . . .": ibid., 162.

"Fear. They weren't naturally . . .": Kent Biffle. "Clyde and Bonnie: Terror in the 30's," *Dallas Morning News*, April 27, 1963.

"made living a humble life . . .": Davis. *Bonnie & Clyde & Me*, 172.

"It would be completely accurate . . .": Hinton. *Ambush*, 104.

"she never fired . . .": Jones. "Riding with Bonnie and Clyde," 162.

"preferred to work alone" and "Smooth Smith": E. J. Dowd. "Memorandum for the File," US Bureau of Investigation #26-4114-120, November 6, 1933, FBI records part 1.

"New Bad Men of the Old . . ." and "lived up to . . .": Lowell M. Limpus. "The New Bad Men of the Old West," *Real Detective*, December 1933, 26.

"Boys, it will take you to midnight . . .": "Shaking With Fear," November 26, 1933.

LEGEND HAS IT: WAS W. D. REALLY HANDCUFFED TO CLYDE?

"He used different methods of being alert": Biffle, interview with W. D. Jones.

15. EASTHAM FARM, TEXAS PRISON SYSTEM, JANUARY 16, 1934.—

"A newsboy once said to his buddy. . . .": Fortune. *Fugitives*, 249.

Mullins was sometimes spelled Mullens and Mullin.

"Hamilton is as gentle . . .": "Prison Officials, Warmed of Hamilton's Escape Plot, Ridiculed It, Dallas Men Say," *Dallas Morning News*, January 18, 1934.

"long arm man": Testimony of B. B. Monzingo, State of Texas v. Joe Palmer, CAC 17260, 22.

"Boy, you had better . . .": Testimony of Olin Bozeman, State of Texas v. Joe Palmer, 23.

"spectacular delivery," "perfectly executed," and "two-gun, cigar-smoking woman": "5 Convicts Freed by Clyde Barrow," *New York Times*, January 17, 1934.

"value friendship more than money.": "Reports of Special Agent C. B. Winstead," including statement of W. H. Bybee, US Bureau of Investigation #26-4114-72, March 29, 1934, FBI records part 5, 2.

"I have always taken care of . . ." and "I should have . . .": Erin Blakemore. "Read a Chilling Letter from Bonnie and Clyde," Smithsonian.com, August 29, 2016.

"didn't give me a dog's. . . .": Testimony of Gordon Burns, State of Texas v. Joe Palmer, 31–32.

"The thing for you to do . . .": Simmons. *Assignment Huntsville*, 128.

"It would have been simple . . .": Walter Prescott Webb. *The Texas Rangers: A Century of Frontier Defense*, Austin, Texas.: University of Texas Press, 1965, 541.

LEGEND HAS IT: DEAD OR ALIVE

"dead or alive" and "There is no law in the Bible . . .": "Reward of $1,000 Offered for Clyde," *Dallas Morning News*, February 17, 1934.

"We are attempting to do the very thing . . .": ibid.

MAJOR JOSEPH CROWSON, 1900–1934

"mistreatment to convicts": Barrow. *My Life with Bonnie & Clyde*, 218.

16. GRAPEVINE, TEX., APRIL 1, 1934.—

"They don't think they're too smart or desperate . . .": Fortune. *Fugitives*, 250.

"Let's take 'em": Davis. *Bonnie & Clyde & Marie*, 218.

"I screamed at my husband to hurry. . . .": "Dallas Couple Jesting About Ill-Fated Highway Officers Just Before Double Killing," *Daily Times Herald*, April 2, 1934, from Schmid scrapbook, November 1933–April 1934.

"a cozy home where . . .": "Murder Blasts Romance of Alto Girl, To Wed Slain Officer April 13," *Dallas Morning News*, April 2, 1934.

"Wanted for Murder": R. H. Colvin. "Wanted for Murder," US Bureau of Investigation unnumbered memo, April 9, 1934, FBI records part 4.

"not a man, he's an animal . . .": "Barrow Sought in Wise County," *Dallas Evening Journal*, April 2, 1934, Schmid scrapbook, November 1933–April 1934.

"Where was the governor . . .": "Editorial: The Hunt for Barrow," *Dallas Dispatch*, April 2, 1934, Schmid scrapbook, November 1933–April 1934.

"sorry they had to shoot..." through "...you can tell that": "Clyde Barrow Thinks He's Too Smart to be Caught," *Daily Times Herald*, April 7, 1934.

"You can tell the officers...": H. E. Hollis. US Bureau of Investigation #26-4114-152, April 19, 1934, FBI records part 4, 5.

"told me she wanted me to tell...": "Clyde Barrow Thinks He's Too Smart to be Caught," April 7, 1934.

"I want you to let the public...": "Hamilton Parts Ways With Barrow, He Writes Lawyer, Remitting $100," *Dallas Morning News*, April 9, 1934.

"Bonnie's not a killer" and "the true story...": "Mrs. Barrow Objects to References to Clyde as West Dallas Killer, Says Never Lived in that Section," *Dallas Evening Journal*, April 13, 1934, Schmid scrapbook, April 1934–July 1934.

"may have to kill them...": Floyd Hamilton. *Bonnie, Clyde and Me!*, audio recording, cassette 1, side B, Minneapolis: GreaTapes, 2000.

"Keep him away...": Fortune. *Fugitives*, 240.

"C&B": Dallas Police Department, "Telephone Tap Log: Barrow/Parker Families," Dallas History & Archives, Dallas Public Library, April 28, 1934, 56.

"the kids": Dallas Police Department, "Telephone Tap Log," April 26, 1934, 46.

"I've got a big pot full of beans and some cornbread": ibid., 42.

"the Howards are out here in front and I want to see them before they leave": ibid., April 27, 1934, 48.

"The Howards": Barrow. Author interview.

"Henry": H. E. Hollis. US Bureau of Investigation #26-4114-152, 5.

"had shown signs of unusual and mysterious prosperity": James O. Peyronnin. US Division of Investigation #26-4114-141, April 18, 1934, FBI records part 4, 2.

"a wolf, suspicious and real smart": "Statement of Henderson Jordan to H. Glenn Jordan," October 12, 1958, Texas Prison Museum archives, from the collection of Lorraine Joyner, Caster, LA, donated in 1990.

"on the spot": Letter from R. Whitley to Director, Division of Investigation, April 24, 1934, US Bureau of Investigation #26-4114-157, FBI records part 4, 1.

"wiped out": Letter from R. Whitley to Director, Division of Investigation, April 30, 1934, US Bureau of Investigation #26-4114-166, FBI records part 4, 1.

H. D. MURPHY, 1911–1934, AND EDWARD B. WHEELER, 1907–1934

"petticoat ranger": Joe Simnacher. "Doris Brown Edwards—Obituary," *Dallas Morning News*, June 23, 2007.

"It's like we don't even...": Bud Kennedy. "Easter of Tears," *Fort Worth Star-Telegram*, April 19, 2014.

LEGEND HAS IT: A WEDDING DRESS

"school days brought forth a friendship...": F.L. Weimar. "H. D. Murphy Buried at Old Palestine Thursday," *Alto Herald*, April 15, 1934, accessed from the Portal to Texas History.

CAL CAMPBELL, 1873–1934

"it kept us eating...." through "...help someone": Royko, *For the Love of Mike*, 203–204.

LEGEND HAS IT: CLYDE'S CORRESPONDENCE

"dandy" and "Even if my business . . .": Clyde Barrow letter to Henry Ford, from the collections of the Henry Ford, gift of Ford Motor Company.

"Clyde": Clyde Barrow, letter to Mr. King, "But He Was Not Smart Enough," Texas Ranger Hall of Fame and Museum archives, Armstrong Texas Ranger Research Center, Frank Hamer file, Waco, Texas.

17. NEAR GIBSLAND, LA., MAY 23, 1934.—

"Some day they'll go down together . . .": Fortune. *Fugitives*, 250.

"the finest old couple he ever saw": "Clyde's Dad Certain Gunman was Betrayed by Convict He Aided," *Daily Times Herald*, June 3, 1934.

"while cunning, lack initiative": R. Whitley letter to Division of Investigation director, May 14, 1934, US Bureau of Investigation #26-4114-196, FBI records part 4, 2.

"I feel certain we will sack the gang here": Letter from Frank Hamer to Frank J. Blake, Dallas Agent in Charge, May 11, 1934, US Bureau of Investigation #26-4114-82, FBI records part 7, 5.

"Everyone in this country thinks. . . .": Letter from C. L. Tolbert letter to Capt. S. O. Hamm, Texas State Highway Department, April 13, 1934, US Bureau of Investigation document #26-4114-42, FBI records part 7.

"They was nice to me . . . ": "Told Nothing! Mrs. Barrow Claims as Returned Home," *Dallas Evening Journal*, May 12, 1934, from Schmid scrapbook, April 1934–July 1934.

"unlawful": "Action Not Authorized by Her, Says Governor," *Fort Worth Star Telegram*, May 10, 1934.

"Those tactics are . . .": ibid.

"more than anything . .", R. Whitley letter, May 14, 1934, #26-4114-196, FBI records part 4, 2.

"The old hen is about ready . . .": Simmons. *Assignment Huntsville*, p. 133.

"That's them, boys": Sheriff Henderson Jordan. "Sheriff of Parish Tells How Barrow Drove Into Trap," *Dallas Morning News*, May 24, 1934.

"Like a panther": Phillips. *Running with Bonnie and Clyde*, 206.

"It was just a roar . . .": Bob Alcorn and Ted Hinton. "Took No Chances, Hinton and Alcorn Tell Newspapermen," *Dallas Dispatch*, May 24, 1934, reprint from the Dallas Public Library.

"Halt": ibid.

"Did you sleep good. . . .": ibid.

"It was just gruesome": Mildred Cole Lyons. *Remembering Bonnie and Clyde*, video recording, Valley Park, Mo.: Turquoise Film/Video Productions, 1994.

"I can tell you what happened . . .": "Shot the Devil Out of Them," *New York Times*, May 24, 1934.

"I hated to bust a cap . . .": "50 Bullets Hit Pair," *New York Times*, May 24, 1934.

"Her love of cigars was fact and not fiction": Charles Newell. "Hamer Tells Inside Story of Barrow Hunt," *Dallas Dispatch*, May 25, 1934, reprint.

LEGEND HAS IT: WAS BONNIE PREGNANT?

"is in a delicate condition": Letter from Frank Hamer to Frank J. Blake, May 11, 1934, #26-4114-82, FBI records part 7, 5.

18. DALLAS, TEX.—

"Here Is Story of Bonnie and Clyde . . .": "Here is Story of Bonnie and Clyde . . ." *Daily Times Herald*, May 23, 1934.

"The Story of Bonnie and Clyde": Fortune. *Fugitives*, 247.

"Clyde had her . . .": "Thousands View Body of Barrow But Bonnie Hidden From Public," *The Times* (Shreveport, Louisiana), May 25, 1934.

"They shouted, they stormed. . . .": "30,000 Storm Funeral Homes, Cause $400 Damage in Fight to View Desperadoes' Bodies," *Dallas Evening Journal*, May 25, 1934, Schmid scrapbook.

"I pray God to have mercy on her soul": "Bonnie's Mother Faints," *Dallas Dispatch*, May 27, 1934, Schmid scrapbook.

"Gone but not forgotten" and "As the flowers are all made sweeter . . .": author visit to graves, May 26, 2014.

"been wronged" and "the law made a mistake": "Mrs. Mace Freed When Expert Puts Blame on Barrow," *Dallas Morning News*, June 1, 1934.

"that I might see him alive . . .": "Runs into Trap," *Dallas Morning News*, May 24, 1934.

"a lonely country road" and "shot after shot pouring . . .": Cumie Barrow. Unpublished manuscript.

"The Most Sensational Film Ever Made": Advertisement for the Majestic, *Fort Worth Star-Telegram*, June 1, 1934.

"You can't do that to my boy": "Barrow's Mother Tears Down Photo of Son at Theater," *Dallas Morning News*, May 31, 1934.

"I Saw Clyde Barrow Kill Five Men" through ". . . death train with Barrow": W. D. Jones, as told to Clarke Newlon. "I Saw Clyde Barrow Kill Five Men," *Startling Detective Mysteries*, May 1934, 6–7.

"The Inside Story of 'Bonnie' Parker and 'The Bloody Barrows'": Ed Portley, as told to C. F. Waers. *True Detective Mysteries*, June 1934, 26.

"They were a couple that" through ". . . big black cigars": ibid., 29.

"the greatest indictment known . . .": Fortune. *Fugitives*, 29.

"highly important in the drive . . .": "Eighteen Arrested for Aiding Clyde, Bonnie," *Dallas Morning News*, January 29, 1935.

"He was my boy. . . ." through ". . . one of these?": "Murder of Hamilton Planned by Former Pal, Clyde Barrow," *Dallas Morning News*, February 24, 1935.

"The Constitution never intended" through "this conspiracy": "Fate of Group in Harboring Case to Jury," *Dallas Morning News*, February 26, 1935.

19. HOLLYWOOD, CALIF.—

"You've read the story of Jesse James . . .": Fortune. *Fugitives*, 247.

"I'm going to tell the truth . . .": J. Edgar Hoover. *Persons in Hiding*, Boston: Little, Brown and Company, 1938, xviii.

"Killer in Skirts" and "America's deadliest sweetheart": Marvin H. Albert. "Killer in Skirts," *Argosy*, March 1956, 20.

"weak chin" and "soft hazel eyes": John Toland. *The Dillinger Days*, New York: Random House, 1963, 38.

"had homosexual tendencies": ibid., 39.

"They were, in short . . . ": ibid., 78.

"Everybody in Texas grew up . . .": Harris. *Pictures at a Revolution: Five Movies and the Birth of the New Hollywood*, New York: The Penguin Press, 2008, 12.

"were heroes of a kind . . .": Sandra Wake and Nicola Hayden, compilers and editors. *The Bonnie & Clyde Book*, New York: Simon and Schuster, 1972, 18.

"underworld" and "What we now call . . .": ibid., 19.

"as great romantic figures" through ". . . their humanity": Benton. Author interview, March 30, 2017.

"Who wants to see the rise and fall . . .": Harris. *Pictures at a Revolution*, 195.

"spastic and balletic" and "to do something extraordinary . . .": ibid., 256.

"I don't think the original Bonnie and Clyde . . .": Wake and Hayden. *Bonnie & Clyde Book*, 7.

"It whips through the saga . . .": Bosley Crowther. "Shoot-em-up Film Opens World Fete," *New York Times*, August 7, 1967.

"squalid shoot-'em for the moron trade": Joe Morgenstern. "Two for a Tommy Gun," *Newsweek*, August 21, 1967, 65.

"I felt a cold sweat dripping . . .": Joe Morgenstern. Author interview, August 4, 2015.

"grossly unfair and regrettably . . .": Joe Morgenstern. "The Thin Red Line," *Newsweek*, August 28, 1967, 82.

"The Legend of Bonnie & Clyde": Merle Haggard and the Strangers. "The Legend of Bonnie and Clyde," LP, Capitol Records, 1968.

"my aunt Artie said . . .": Buddy Barrow. Author interview, November 12, 2015.

"My family wanted them to rest in peace": Buddy Barrow, at the Lorraine Joyner Historical Meeting, Gibsland, Louisana, May 20, 2016.

"made me look like a screaming horse's ass": Barrow, *My Life with Bonnie & Clyde*, 181.

BIBLIOGRAPHY

―――――◆―――――

BOOKS

Barrow, Blanche Caldwell, edited by John Neal Phillips. *My Life with Bonnie & Clyde*. Norman, Oklahoma: University of Oklahoma Press, 2004.

Boessenecker, John. *Texas Ranger: The Epic Life of Frank Hamer, the Man Who Killed Bonnie and Clyde*. New York: Thomas Dunne Books, 2016.

Dallas County Sheriff's Department, 1846–1988. Sponsored by the Dallas County Sheriff's Association, Dallas County Sheriff's Posse and Dallas County Sheriff's Reserves. Dallas, Texas: Dallas County Sheriff's Department, 1989.

Davis, Jonathan. *Bonnie & Clyde & Marie: A Sister's Perspective on the Notorious Barrow Gang*. Nacogdoches, Texas: Stephen F. Austin State University Press, 2014.

Fortune, Jan I., editor. *Fugitives: The Story of Clyde Barrow and Bonnie Parker as Told by Bonnie's Mother (Mrs. Emma Parker) and Clyde's Sister (Nell Barrow Cowan)*. Reprint. Fort Worth, Texas: Wild Horse Press, 2013.

Guinn, Jeff. *Go Down Together: The True, Untold Story of Bonnie & Clyde*. New York, New York: Simon and Schuster, 2009.

Harris, Mark. *Pictures at a Revolution: Five Movies and the Birth of the New Hollywood*. New York, New York: The Penguin Press, 2008.

Hill, Patricia Evridge. *Dallas: The Making of a Modern City*. Austin, Texas: University of Texas Press, 1996.

Hinton, Ted, as told to Larry Grove. *Ambush: The Real Story of Bonnie and Clyde*. Fredericksburg, Texas: Shoal Creek Publishers, Inc., 1979.

Hoover, J. Edgar. *Persons in Hiding*. Boston, Massachusetts: Little, Brown and Company, 1938.

Knight, James R., with Jonathan Davis. *Bonnie and Clyde: A Twenty-First Century Update*. Austin, Texas: Eakin Press, 2003.

Kyvig, David E. *Daily Life in the United States, 1920–1940: How Americans Lived Through the "Roaring Twenties" and the Great Depression*. Chicago, Illinois: Ivan R. Dee, 2002.

Lachenmayer, Tom. *History of the Dallas Police Department*. December 10, 1974. Dallas History & Archives, Dallas Public Library.

Phillips, John Neal. *Running with Bonnie and Clyde: The Ten Fast Years of Ralph Fults*. Norman, Oklahoma: University of Oklahoma Press, 1996.

Ramsey, Winston G., editor. *On the Trail of Bonnie & Clyde, Then and Now*. London: Battle of Britain International Ltd., 2003.

Schneider, Paul. *Bonnie and Clyde: The Lives Behind the Legend*. New York, New York: Henry Holt and Company, 2009.

Simmons, Lee. *Assignment Huntsville: Memoirs of a Texas Prison Official*. Austin, Texas: University of Texas Press, 1957.

Toland, John. *The Dillinger Days*. New York, New York: Random House, 1963.

Treherne, John. *The Strange History of Bonnie and Clyde*. New York, New York: Stein and Day, 1984.

Underwood, Sid. *Depression Desperado: The Chronicle of Raymond Hamilton*. Austin, Texas: Eakin Press, 1995.

Wake, Sandra and Nicola Hayden, editors. *The Bonnie and Clyde Book*. New York, New York: Simon & Schuster, 1967.

Webb, Walter Prescott. *The Texas Rangers: A Century of Frontier Defense*. Austin, Texas: University of Texas Press, 1965.

MAGAZINE AND JOURNAL ARTICLES AND OTHER DOCUMENTS

Albert, Marvin II. "Killer in Skirts." *Argosy*, March 1956, 20–21, 80–85.

Barrow, Clyde. Letter from Clyde Barrow to Henry Ford Praising the Ford V-8 Car, 1934. The Henry Ford, gift of Ford Motor Company. Accessed online.

Barrow, Clyde. Letter to Mr. King: "But He Was Not Smart Enough." Texas Ranger Hall of Fame and Museum archives, Armstrong Texas Ranger Research Center, Frank Hamer file, Waco, Texas.

Barrow, Cumie. Unpublished, unpaged manuscript. Bonnie & Clyde Research Collection, box 2, folder 6, East Texas Research Center, Ralph W. Steen Library, Stephen F. Austin State University.

Blakemore, Erin. "Read a Chilling Letter from Bonnie and Clyde." Smithsonian.com, August, 291, 2016.

Quiver, Carolyn. "A Day With Bonnie and Clyde." *North Louisiana Historical Association Journal*, Winter 1971, accessed via America, History & Life database.

Crumbaker, Marge. "Bonnie, Clyde and 2 Who Remember Them." *Texas Tempo*, May 1968. Bonnie and Clyde Research Collection, box 2, folder 39, East Texas Research Center, Ralph W. Steen Library, Stephen F. Austin State University.

Dallas Police Department. "Telephone Tap Log: Barrow/Parker Families." Dallas History & Archives, Dallas Public Library.

Dickson, Paul and Thomas B. Allen. "Marching on History," Smithsonian com, February 2003.

Eslick, Louis E. "Report of Raid at Thirty-fourth and Oakridge Drive." Missouri State Highway Patrol, April 14, 1933. Courtesy of Paul Schneider.

Johns, Joe, submitted by Eve Ball. "Kidnapped by Bandits." *True West*, September 1981. Bonnie and Clyde Research Collection, box 2, folder 26, Ralph W. Steen Library, Stephen F. Austin State University.

Jones, W. D., as told to Clarke Newlon. "I Saw Clyde Barrow Kill Five Men." *Startling Detective Mysteries*, May and June 1934.

Jones, W. D. "Riding with Bonnie & Clyde." *Playboy*, November 1968. Dallas History & Archives, "Bonnie and Clyde, 1960–1969" folder, Dallas Public Library.

Jordan, Sheriff Henderson, as told to C. F. Waers. "The Inside Story of the Killing of 'Bonnie' Parker and Clyde Barrow." *True Detective Mysteries*, November 1934.

Lamm, Michael. "Henry Ford's Last Mechanical Triumph." *Special-Interest Autos #21*, March–April 1974, 13–19, 55–56.

Limpus, Lowell M. "The New Bad Men of the Old West." *Real Detective*, December 1933.

McCormick, Harry. Scrapbook. Dallas History & Archives, Dallas Public Library.

Morgenstern, Joe. "The Thin Red Line." *Newsweek*, August 28, 1967, 82–83.

Morgenstern, Joe. "Two for a Tommy Gun." *Newsweek*, August 21, 1967, 65.

Phillps, John Neal, and Ralph Fults. "The Man Who Ran with Bonnie and Clyde." *Dallas Life Magazine*, June 10, 1984.

Portley, Ed, as told to C. F. Waers. "The Inside Story of 'Bonnie' Parker and 'The Bloody Barrows.'" *True Detective Mysteries*, June, July, August, September, October, 1934.

Rich, Carroll Y. "The Autopsy of Bonnie and Clyde." *Western Folklore Society*, January 1970, 27–33.

Schmid, Sheriff R. A. "Smoot." Scrapbooks, 1933–1935. Dallas History & Archives, Dallas Public Library.

"Statement of Henderson Jordan to H. Glenn Jordan," Texas Prison Museum archives, October 12, 1958. From the collection of Lorraine Joyner, Caster, Louisiana.

State of Texas v. Joe Palmer. CAC 17260. Texas State Library and Archives, Austin, Texas.

"The Line Up." *True Detective Mysteries*, May 1933 and September 1933.

"To Serve & Protect: A Collection of Memories." Missouri State Highway Patrol, Public Information and Education Division, 2006. Accessed online.

Veit, Richard J. "The Waco Jailbreak of Bonnie and Clyde." *Waco Heritage and History*, December 1990, 3–20.

Williams, Francis. "The Day Bonnie and Clyde Shot It Out With the Law in Ferrelview." *Discover North*, March 1974. Bonnie and Clyde Research Collection, box 1, folder 14, East Texas Research Center, Ralph W. Steen Library, Stephen F. Austin State University.

NEWSPAPER ARTICLES

DAILY CURRENT-ARGUS (CARLSBAD, N.MEX.)

Johns, Joe. "Former Eddy County Sheriff Writes Own Complete Story of Wild Rid with Bandits." *Daily Current-Argus*, August 17, 1932.

"Local Deputy Sheriff Safe in San Antonio; Desperados Escape." *Daily Current-Argus,* August 15, 1932.

DAILY TIMES HERALD/DALLAS TIMES HERALD

"Barrow and Girl Pal Won't Be Taken Alive, Former Partner Says." *Daily Times Herald*, July 26, 1933.

"Bullets Await Barrow Boys in Texas." *Daily Times Herald,* April 14, 1933.

"Clyde Barrow Thinks He's Too Smart to Be Caught." *Daily Times Herald*, April 7, 1934.

"Clyde's Dad Certain Gunman Was Betrayed by Convict He Aided." *Daily Times Herald*, June 3, 1934.

De Shong, Andrew. "Mothers of Two West Dallas Outlaws Fearful for Future." *Daily Times Herald*, January 10, 1933.

"Here is Story of Bonnie and Clyde Penned By Gungirl Before She Died Asking for Burial—Side by Side." *Daily Times Herald*, May 23, 1934.

M'Bride, Pierce. "Bonnie Parker's Demand for Share of Bank Loot Cause of Clyde Barrow-Hamilton Split." *Daily Times Herald*, April 19, 1934.

M'Bride, Pierce. "Clyde's Dad Certain Gunman Was Betrayed by Convict He Aided." *Daily Times Herald*, June 3, 1934.

Muller, Bill. "Ex-gangster Only One Left to Tell Tale of Bonnie, Clyde." *Dallas Times Herald*, July 5, 1991.

"Pair Wanted for Slayings Sought in Texas Holdups." *Daily Times Herald*, August 8, 1932.

"Police Expect Early Arrest of 2 Killers." *Daily Times Herald*, August 9, 1932.

"Two Women Charged After Deputy Slain." *Daily Times Herald*, January 7, 1933.

DALLAS MORNING NEWS

Alcorn, Bob. "Dallas Deputy Tells of Ending Long Chase." *Dallas Morning News*, May 24, 1934.

"Bandits Leave No Trail After $440 Robbery." *Dallas Morning News,* August 2, 1932.

"Barrow Boys Take 2 Officers Captive After Car Crashes." *Dallas Morning News*, June 12, 1933.

"Barrow's Mother Tears Down Photo of Son at Theater." *Dallas Morning News*, May 31, 1934.

Biffle, Kent. "Clyde and Bonnie: Terror in the 30's." *Dallas Morning News*, April 27, 1963.

Bullock, Helen. "Of Hattie Rankin Moore, Who Loved West Dallas." *Dallas Morning News*, October 7, 1951.

"City's Sewage Fouls Trinity for 150 Miles." *Dallas Morning News*, September 14, 1929.

Crozier, Harry Benge. "Prison Not Fit for Dog Moody Informs House." *Dallas Morning News*, January 30, 1930.

"Deputy Not Slain." *Dallas Morning News*, August 16, 1932.

"Eighteen Arrested for Aiding Clyde, Bonnie." *Dallas Morning News,* January 29, 1935.

"Fate of Group in Harboring Case to Jury." *Dallas Morning News,* February 16, 1935.

"Hamilton Parts Ways with Barrow, He Writes Lawyer, Remitting $100." *Dallas Morning News,* April 9, 1934.

"He's My Boy, Sobs Barrow's Mother; I Want to See Him." *Dallas Morning News*, July 25, 1933.

"How 'Smoot' Schmid Got His Nickname." *Dallas Morning News*, August 28, 1932.

Jordan, Sheriff Henderson. "Sheriff of Parish Tells How Barrow Drove Into Trap." *Dallas Morning News*, May 24, 1934.

"Man Hunt Gets Hot as Dallas Seeks Gunmen." *Dallas Morning News*, August 9, 1932.

"Mother Hugs Belief Her Boys Not Killers as Older Sons Hunted." *Dallas Morning News*, April 15, 1933.

"Mrs. Mace Freed When Expert Puts Blame on Barrow." *Dallas Morning News*, June 1, 1934.

"Murder Blasts Romance of Alto Girl, To Wed Slain Officer April 13." *Dallas Morning News*, April 2, 1934.

"Murder of Hamilton Planned by Former Pal, Clyde Barrow." *Dallas Morning News*, February 24, 1935.

Pederson, Rena. "Badmen's Pal 'Outgrowed' Wild Life." *Dallas Morning News*, March 28, 1976.

"Pretty Boy is New Suspect in Killing; Jesse James Next." *Dallas Morning News*, January 20, 1933.

"Prison Officials, Warmed of Hamilton's Escape Plot, Ridiculed It, Dallas Men Say." *Dallas Morning News*, January 18, 1934.

"Reward of $1,000 Offered for Clyde." *Dallas Morning News*, February 17, 1934.

"Relief for Itinerant Campers to Be Sought at Charities Meeting." *Dallas Morning News*, February 21, 1923.

"Runs into Trap." *Dallas Morning News*, May 24, 1934.

Simnacher, Joe. "Doris Brown Edwards—Obituary." *Dallas Morning News*, June 23, 2007.

"Shaking With Fear, Prisoner Tells of More Barrow Killings." *Dallas Morning News*, November 26, 1933.

Tolbert, Frank X. "Taken for a Ride by Bonnie and Clyde." *Dallas Morning News*, March 18, 1968.

"Tough 2-Gun Girl with Desperadoes Who Killed Davis." *Dallas Morning News*, January 13, 1933.

DES MOINES REGISTER

Grant, Donald. "Posse Plans Attack Today To Seize Trio." *Des Moines Register*, July 25, 1933.

Grant, Donald. "Trail Is Cold in Gang Hunt." *Des Moines Register*, July 26, 1933.

Hullihan, Robert. "When an Iowa Shootin' Fool Met 'Bloody Barrows.'" *Des Moines Register*, October 26, 1975.

"Mother Hopes Clyde Barrow Is Out of State." *Des Moines Register*, July 27, 1933.

"Mrs. Barrow Feared Fight Was 'The End.'" *Des Moines Register*, July 25, 1933.

ELECTRA NEWS

"Bandit Trio Kidnaps Three; Two Take Them for Ride." *Electra News*, April 14, 1932.

"W. N. Owens Held 12 Hours Thursday by Two Kidnapers." *Electra News*, April 21, 1932.

FORT WORTH STAR-TELEGRAM

"Action Not Authorized by Her, Says Governor." *Fort Worth Star-Telegram*, May 13, 1934.

Advertisement for the Majestic. *Fort Worth Star-Telegram*, June 1, 1934.

Kennedy, Bud. "Easter of Tears." *Fort Worth Star-Telegram*, April 19, 2014.

"Many Officers Join Hunt for Deputy Slayers." *Fort Worth Star-Telegram*, January 8, 1933.

"Third Woman Quizzed in Deputy Killing." *Fort Worth Star-Telegram*, January 9, 1933.

Utecht, Byron C. "Many Persons Asked Clemency for Barrow." *Fort Worth Star-Telegram,* January 19, 1934.

JOPLIN GLOBE

Brothers, Kit. "Policeman Kidnapped by Barrows Dies at 81." *Joplin Globe*, July 27, 1989.

"Desperados Kill Two Officers Here." *Joplin Globe*, April 14, 1933.

"M'Ginnis Was Popular as a Peace Officer." *Joplin Globe*, April 15, 1933.

NEW YORK TIMES

"5 Convicts Freed by Clyde Barrow." *New York Times*, January 17, 1934.

"50 Bullets Hit Pair." *New York Times*, May 24, 1934.

Crowther, Bosley. "Shoot-Em-Up Film Opens World Fete." *New York Times*, August 7, 1967.

"Shot the Devil Out of Them." *New York Times*, May 24, 1934.

"Uncle Sam Presses His New War on Crime." *New York Times*, August 20, 1933.

WACO NEWS-TRIBUNE

"Baby Thug a Killer?" *Waco News-Tribune*, March 29, 1930.

"Jail Break Plot Fails." *Waco News-Tribune*, March 27, 1930.

"Jailers Held Up With Pistol; Prisoners Escape." *Waco News-Tribune*, March 12, 1930.

"Mrs. Barrow Blames Bad Companions for Downfall of Her 'Baby Thug' Son." *Waco News-Tribune*, March 28, 1930.

WACO TIMES-HERALD

"'Baby Thug' Faces Murder Charge." *Waco Times-Herald*, March 25, 1930.

"'Baby Thugs' Get Long Terms." *Waco Times-Herald*, March 24, 1930.

OTHERS

Associated Press. "Wellington Officers Say Barrow Pair Abductors." *Amarillo Daily News*, June 12, 1933.

"Atoka County Officers Fall Victims of Bandits Guns at Stringtown, Friday Night." 1932 news story reproduced in the *Atoka Indian Citizen*, June 24, 1992.

"Bandits Raid Lucerne." *Pharos-Tribune* (Logansport, Indiana), May 12, 1933.

Darby, H. D. "Darby Relates Details of His Ride with Kidnapers." *Ruston Daily Leader*, April 28, 1933.

Gast, Dorothy. "Bonnie and Clyde No Heroes, Victim Says." *Kansas City Star*, September 17, 1978.

"Kidnappers of Local Officers Still at Large." *Wellington Leader*, June 15, 1933.

Newell, Charles. "Hamer Tells Inside Story of Barrow Hunt." *Dallas Dispatch*, May 25, 1934, reprint edition.

Redden, Mamie. "More About Barrow, Hamilton, and the Death of Gene Moore." *Atoka County Times*, March 28, 1968.

Rogers, Rob. "A Life Remembered: Brush with Famed Gunman Changed His Life." *News-Review* (Roseburg, Oregon), November 21, 2003.

Royko, Mike. "The Real Bonnie and Clyde Left a Trail of Lingering Sorrow." *Des Moines Tribune*, February 24, 1968.

"Shanghai Sheriff After Gun Fight Over Stolen Car." *Las Vegas Daily Optic* (New Mexico), August 15, 1932.

"Thousands View Body of Barrow But Bonnie Hidden from Public." *The Times* (Shreveport, Lousiana), May 25, 1934.

Waco's Dumbell Bandits, Captured in Ohio, Back in M'Lennan County Jail." *Waco Sunday Tribune*, March 23, 1930.

Weimar, F. L. "H. D. Murphy Buried at Old Palestine Thursday." *Alto Herald*, April 15, 1934.

RECORDINGS

Biffle, Kent. Interview with W. D. Jones, June 1969, on cassette, transferred to CD. Kent Biffle Papers, box 55, Special Collections, University of Texas at Arlington.

Bonnie and Clyde. DVD. Burbank, California.: Warner Bros. Pictures, 1967.

Collins, Jud, interviewer. *The Truth About Bonnie and Clyde, as told by Billie Jean Parker (Bonnie's Sister)*. New York, New York: RCA Victor, 1968., album, converted to digital.

Haggard, Merle, and the Strangers. "The Legend of Bonnie and Clyde." LP, Capitol Records, 1968.

Hamilton, Floyd. *Bonnie and Clyde and Me!*, four cassette audio recording. Minneapolis: GreaTapes, 2000.

Ralph Fults Tells His Story with Bonnie and Clyde. Southwest Historical Inc. Transcript courtesy of Paul Schneider.

"Remembering Bonnie & Clyde." DVD. Valley Park, Missouri: Turquoise Film/Video Productions, 1994.

INTERNET RESOURCES

BonnieAndClydeHistory.com: bonnieandclydehistory.blogspot.com

Dallas Municipal Archives. "Clyde Barrow Gang Collection." Accessed through the Portal to Texas History, University of North Texas: texashistory.unt.edu/explore/collections/BCM/browse

Debez.com: blanche.debez.com

Henry Methvin: tmethvin.com/henry

Texashideout.com: texashideout.tripod.com/bc.htm

US Bureau of Investigation. "Bonnie and Clyde." *FBI Records: The Vault.* Seven parts. Accessed at: vault. fbi.gov/Bonnie%20and%20Clyde

Wellington, Texas, website: wellingtontx.com/9578158_88485.htm

West Dallas Neighborhood Development Corporation. "West Dallas Environmental History": senate.state. tx.us/members/d23/westdal/index.htm

AUTHOR INTERVIEWS

Baker, Terry, retired Dallas County sheriff, July 23, 2015.

Barrow, Buddy, stepson of L. C. Barrow, August 17, 2015, and November 12, 2015.

Benton, Robert, screenwriter, *Bonnie and Clyde*, March 30, 2017.

Davis, Chris, Cherokee County judge, November 7, 2016.

Davis, Jonathan, August 8, 2015, and October 24, 2015.

Fine, Dr. Lauren, emergency room physician, September 14, 2016.

McBurney, John, national chief judge, Early Ford V-8 Club of America, February 27, 2017, and by email.

Morgenstern, Joe, former *Newsweek* film critic, August 4, 2015.

Singletary, Virginia, Alto, Texas, librarian, November 7, 2016.

Slate, John, city of Dallas archivist, June 22, 2015, and September 15, 2015.

PHOTO CREDITS

Title page: Library of Congress, Prints & Photographs Division, NYWT&S Collection; Prologue, 132, 186: AP Images; 3, 184: Courtesy of John Neal Phillips; 11: Courtesy of Jonathan Davis; 15: Courtesy of Dallas Historical Society. Used by permission; 17, 34, 47, 88, 113–114, 143, 195: Courtesy of Buddy Barrow; 18, 20: General Photograph Collection, UTSA Special Collections; 23–24, 29, 59, 85–86, 94, 140, 158, 174, 185, 188, 194, 203 (bottom): Dallas History & Archives division, Dallas Public Library; 37 (top): Texas Prison Museum, Lee Simmons Collection, 37 (bottom): Texas Prison Museum, Huntsville, Tex.; 40: Texas Convict and Conduct Registers, Texas State Library and Archives Commission, via Ancestry.com; 53: © Karen Blumenthal; 56, 109, 126: Texas Prison Museum, John Neal Phillips Collection; 57: *After the Battle*; 63, 77, 106, 145, 189: Courtesy of Dallas Municipal Archives; 68: The Atoka County Historical Society & Museum; 73, 171: From the Collections of The Henry Ford; 82: FBI and TexasHideout. tripod.com; 92: Courtesy of Tarrant County Sheriff's Office; 99: Courtesy of Kent Biffle Papers, Special Collections, University of Texas at Arlington Libraries, Arlington, Tex.; 103: Courtesy of Jim Hounschell; 105: Composite photo, left to right, from the *Evening News* (Wilkes-Barre, Pa.), *Daily Press* (Newport News, Va.), *Dallas Dispatch*, *Fresno Bee-Republican*, and *Ruston (La.) Daily Leader*; 121: Courtesy of James R. Knight; 134, 136: From the *Des Moines Register*, July 26, 1933, © 1933, Gannet-Community Publishing. All rights reserved. Used by permission and protected by the Copyright Laws of the United States. The printing, copying, redistribution, or retransmission of this Content without express written permission is prohibited; 148, 160: Courtesy of the Patton family; 153: Courtesy of RR Auction; 155: Courtesy of the Texas Ranger Hall of Fame and Museum, Waco, Tex.; 156: Texas Prison Museum, Pierce Collection; 161: Courtesy of Texas Department of Public Safety; 164–165: *The Oklahoman*; 203 (top): Courtesy of Everett Collection.

INDEX